D1714160

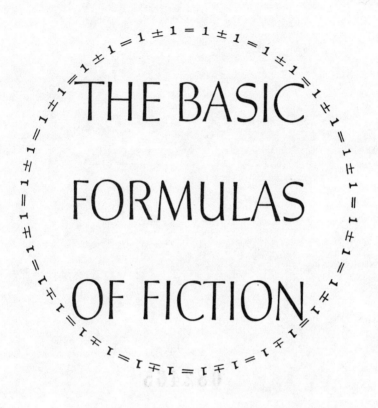

THE BASIC FORMULAS OF FICTION

FOSTER-HARRIS

UNIVERSITY OF OKLAHOMA PRESS

NORMAN

International Standard Book Number: 0-8061-0135-0

Library of Congress Catalog Card Number: 60-7740

Copyright 1944, 1960 by the University of Oklahoma Press, Publishing Division of the University. Manufactured in the U.S.A. First edition, 1944; second printing, 1945; third printing, 1947; fourth printing, 1952; revised edition, entirely reset and reprinted, 1960; second printing of the new edition, 1963; third printing of the new edition, 1967; fourth printing of the new edition, 1973; fifth printing of the new edition, 1977.

To My Mother . . .

Where she went in this world she made of herself no trouble—instead she pitched in and helped

Apologia pro Vita Mea

Dear Editor:

You have told me to avoid an introduction, since to do so is to follow the modern way for both writers and readers. But instinct tells me that the old, traditional way is perhaps best—at least in this instance. It is bad enough to dress an old idea in new clothes, but to offer a new idea in new clothes requires forewarning.

And you have told me to use logical organization. But I don't like what passes for logic today, nor can I find any use for it in giving to others what I have practiced myself, namely, the methods for writing fiction that sells. In all truth, I have taught students most illogically, and with similar irreverence for logic they have sold, surprisingly, to all kinds of markets, both high and low. I can claim only the pragmatic sanction.

This way works. And, after all, what is logic? "Logic," says John Stuart Mill, "is not the science of belief, but the science of proof." In fiction, we are not concerned with proving anything. If we were, the result might not—probably would not—be fiction. I exclude from this, of course, the classic syllogisms in the conversations on foreign language between Huck Finn and Miss Watson's Nigger Jim.

If this book proves to be the simplest one on fiction writing you have ever read, I shall be glad. For twenty years I have been reading about fiction formulas. Sad to relate, however, I have never been able to find the formulas themselves in the dissertations of others. I used to think that my failure to get at the formulas was due to my ignorance of the differential calculus in which other analysts wrote. But when I asked them about the applications of a simpler mathematics—one plus one—they seemed not to know. It was a shock.

Well, here the formulas are. This, insofar as I have been able to determine, is the first book to state them in the baldest, simplest form to which they can be reduced. If you were able to master first-grade arithmetic, you can master these equations. You can not only see them for yourself, but you can pull them out of nine-tenths of the modern short fiction you read. I have not only made them as simple as $1 + 1 = 2$, I have made them $1 + 1 = 2$!

Here, also for the first time, is the *way* that must be followed in creating a story. This way is, of course, somewhat more difficult to master and make your own than is the mere recognition of fiction formulas. Yet, it is no more difficult to apply than it is to apply schoolroom arithmetic to the real problems for which arithmetic was devised. I will admit frankly that there are other ways, just as there are other arithmetics and other geometries. But this one is, I believe, the simplest thus far.

I have included other information which will be useful, I trust, even though it may not be unique, to the end that this book may be as complete a manual as possible for beginning writers. And perhaps I had better add one final warning—on style.

Book editors (you among them) are logical and objective in their thinking. Very well. But this book is deliberately not logical or objective. You may be somewhat puzzled about its style until the *way* begins to be apparent. The idea is, you supply the patience, I supply the way. Or would you call it waywardness?

My task has been to turn the natural order of objective exposition inside out and backwards, so that, with persistence, the student eventually will learn this opposite way of fiction. The method is analogous to, and quite as easy as, the procedure followed by an editor or printer in reading type: he sees it reversed and upside down in type galleys or forms. Having o.k.'d it, he knows that the ultimate reader will find it right side up, forward, and correct on the printed page. The writer faces the same general problem.

He must realize that writing is the opposite of reading. As writer, he is just the reverse of the reader. To do his writing job properly, he must learn to "see" the story in reverse, just as an editor or printer must learn to read type direct.

This, I hope, will clarify my use of fictional method in a strictly expository book. It may prove to be a highly useful overtone, revealing by its example a good deal of the technique that is fiction writing. And any reader, I suppose, will realize that I deal principally with the short story simply because that is now the basic form of fiction.

Foster-Harris

Norman, Oklahoma

Contents

xi

The Basic Formulas of Fiction

What A Story Is

Then to the rolling Heav'n itself I cried,
Asking, "What lamp had Destiny to guide
    Her little Children stumbling in the Dark?"
And—"A blind understanding!" Heav'n replied.

RUBAIYAT OF OMAR KHAYYAM

A modern short story is a solved illustration of a problem in moral arithmetic.

It is a parable depicting applied moral principles, just as in the parables of the Bible. Its basic pattern ordinarily is a simple arithmetical equation. Usually this equation is no more elaborate than $1 + 1 = 2$, or $1 - 1 = 0$, the very first patterns for solving problems in tangible things that you learned in first-grade arithmetic. Its so-called "unity," or "unified effect," is obtained simply by sticking to the statement and solution of the problem at hand, obtaining a correct, unit-sum answer.

The reader is satisfied by a good story in precisely the same way you are satisfied when someone begins by saying, "Now I am going to try to add one and one," then writes down $1 + 1 = ?$ then finally substitutes for the question mark the answer, 2.

If our imaginary mathematician had followed his opening statement of the problem by writing down $1 + 14 - 37 + 4$ goats $+ 3.1416$, undoubtedly you would have begun to suspect that he knew not whereof he spoke. And if he had then obtained an "answer" of 17 cows, or πr^2, or even 2, you would have felt a certain dissatisfaction with the proceedings. No? Why?

Why? Because you know instinctively by now the *right* way to set up a $1 + 1 = ?$ problem, and you know also the *right* answer. You were caught at the tender age of six or thereabouts and taught the patterns and tenets of the arithmetical faith. And now, in your old age, you neither question nor depart therefrom.

Down underneath, you also know the "right" and "wrong" of a story, too, else you would not know whether the story pleased you. True, you may not know just *why* you are pleased or displeased. You have not been taught fictional arithmetic as you have been taught factual figures. But they are so similar, these two kinds of arithmetic, that once you have caught the idea, it is as easy for you to "see" the pattern in correct fiction as it is in common problems in real things.

To make the transfer from ordinary arithmetic to the fictional kind, we should be sure that we agree on what ordinary arithmetic is and how we use it.

What is a number, by the way? When you write a "1," what do you mean?

A number is an abstraction of a real thing, or a sum of similar real things. Since, obviously, there cannot be an abstract "real" thing, that is apparently foolishness to begin with. But "impossible" or not, through experience we have discovered that there is a validity and worth to arithmetic. You believe it. And you believe so implicitly that, with it, you produce quite satisfactory works. Yet consider, please, what your first-grade teacher really did when she inculcated in you this perfect faith:

Starting to teach the first equation of mathematics, $1 + 1 = 2$, she knew very well that six-year-old minds could not grasp any such concept as that of a real nothing, an abstract tangibility. So she illustrated her intangible equation with tangible things—apples, for familiar example. She placed two apples on the desk and said brightly,

"Look, now, children! One apple [touching one] plus one apple [touching the other] equals two apples [holding them both up together]."

Ah, yes. But it is not so!

You will have noticed that, first, she said, at least by implication, that *any* one apple plus *any* one apple exactly equals *any* two apples. But, if you try trading two little ones for two big ones down at your fruit stand, you will quickly discover reality.

Further, and still worse, the "2" answer is not two separate "1" apples. Instead, it is a unit, an amalgamation by some sort of magic, of the two "1" apples into a single apple of the "2" order—a unit apple, that is, twice as big, as luscious, as colorful, and as tasty as either of the "1" apples. Can you really do that with real apples?

You cannot, and you know it, despite your persistent feeling that, nevertheless, I am talking nonsense. Captured at the age of six and taught the arithmetical faith all through the years, you just will believe, despite and regardless. And you are right! Intuitively or otherwise, you know that I am confusing pattern and problem, mixing up my tools and the particular job at hand. You realize that "$1 + 1 = 2$" is not inherently linked with apples or elephants or anything else real; that, aside from being so many marks on blackboard or paper, the equation has no tangible reality.

Instead, it is just a method, a pattern, a way of seeing and solving certain problems concerned with real things. It works quite well. But nevertheless, what you apply at the "equals" sign, the principle of addition, you take on blind faith. You have never, nor will you ever, see two real "1" apples actually merged into one real "2" apple.

Perhaps you have never before appreciated what a godlike contribution the men who originated addition and subtraction made to human progress. They gave us a mental tool, an invisible yet potent way that is magnificent in its simplicity, effectiveness, and potentialities. And this idea, please note, is an intangible—something not to be seen as you see the apples. And now, if you still have not quite fathomed what I am driving at, then read once more what I have said about the apples and equations.

Now let us transfer this identical mathematical idea to the problems of fiction.

At least three-fourths of all modern, commercial short fiction and a thundering percentage of the longer stories, too, are written on an elementary $1 + 1 = 2$ or a $1 - 1 = 0$ pattern. Presently, as you grasp the idea, you may prove this for yourself. The $1 + 1$ equation is the popular, or "happy-ending," pattern quite sensibly preferred by at least two-thirds of your potential fiction markets (including all the highest paying ones), while $1 - 1$ is the usual level of erudition displayed in the so-called "quality" magazines.

Practically all fiction writers work by ear, of course, and so may resent my assertion that they do use formulas, indeed, formulas ordinarily as simple as $1 + 1$ and $1 - 1$. Yet, the truth of this analysis is easily determinable. Here is how you go about it:

Since fiction is not concerned with real things at all, but instead with the emotions arising from these things (and people, too, of course), you begin by substituting for abstractions of objective things (corresponding to the numbers in an arithmetical equation) the almost equally abstract names of subjective things, that is, emotions or emotional states.

Thus, in place of "real" arithmetic's $1 + 1 = ?$, you may have, for example, the good fictional problem, *love + honor = ?*

Or, perhaps you may decide to make your problem *security + love = ?* Or *gratitude + hate = ?* Or *selfish-*

ness + love; or *mother love + patriotism (love of country).* Or any of an almost infinite number of other possible combinations.

You must remember that, in addition to the simple emotions, love, hate, fear, courage, and so on, you have a truly tremendous spread of conditioned emotions. *Sacred love + profane love = ?* for illustration, is a venerable love-story formula, a conflict between two kinds of the same emotion, namely love. Or our *security + love* formula above is really a conditioned emotional conflict between love of safety and romantic love. *Mother love + patriotism* is another such. To make a strong story, you need a strong conflict between two emotions. But remembering that, you can match simple emotions against simple ones, conditioned emotions against conditioned ones, or simple against conditioned. It will still be story.

To make this formula idea even more simple, you may read the plus or minus sign between your two factors simply as "versus," if you wish. But I like the arithmetical signs better. After all, arithmetical signs not only indicate that there is a problem—a conflict between the two factors they link—but they also state the nature of the problem and forecast the outcome.

That fictional "answer," by the way, ordinarily is a true ineffable, a condition, I mean, which we know very well but simply cannot put into sharply definitive words. In the happy-ending, "plus" story, it is ecstasy, complete satisfaction, final adjustment, the goal, nirvana, heaven, or whatever similar term you care to use. In the "minus" story, it is hades, purgatory, fitting punishment, or, again, any similar term you prefer. I have not tried to coin any fictional equivalents of the arithmetical "sum" for addition and "remainder" for subtraction.

In our current state of highly scientific materialism, we almost never encounter fiction which applies a formula

7

more complicated than simple addition or subtraction, so plus and minus are all we shall use here. There are stories in which a sort of rudimentary multiplication or division can be detected, but they are so rare, abstruse, or generally unpopular that we may safely ignore them. Not one selling writer in a score ever uses—or perhaps even knows—more than simple plus and minus, while many writers, even famous ones, never learn but the one or the other. You do not have to know much mathematics to be an author.

But, to get on, notice particularly at this point that our fictional equation—*piety + parental love = ?* for example —does not immediately and inevitably suggest any particular people, places, or circumstances. Any more than "$1 + 1 = ?$" inevitably refers to apples and the teacher's desk. Nor is this equation, in the active sense, the solution of any real problem to which it may be applied.

Instead, it is simply the pattern, the set way, whereby a living person may work out an appropriate problem with which he is confronted. Fictional formula, I mean, no more finds the problems for you and solves them while you sleep than "$1 + 1 = 2$" finds oranges or anything else and automatically adds them up without effort on your part. In fictional as in real arithmetic, your equations are simply your tools, and you must do the work with them yourself.

Now to set up our problems, *piety + parental love = ?* so that we may "see" it. We have to give form to our abstractions with apples, better still, with "real" people and "real" things.

"Johnny went to the store and the grocer gave him a nice, shiny apple. Oh, wasn't Johnny pleased! Then the butcher gave him an apple, too. How many apples did Johnny have?"

It's a parable illustrating, to the best of our human ability, one of the great eternal principles that cannot be put exactly in words, one of the ineffable ways that cannot be named. We do the same with our fiction problem.

I have chosen for my illustrating equation perhaps the finest example of the $1+1=2$ story we have in literature, the twenty-second chapter of Genesis. This, if you are old-fashioned enough to remember it, relates the testing of Abraham by the Lord.

> And it came to pass after these things, that God did tempt Abraham, and said unto him, Abraham: and he said, Behold, *here I am*.
> And he said, Take now thy son, thine only *son* Isaac, whom thou lovest, and get thee into the land of Moriah; and offer him there for a burnt offering upon one of the mountains which I will tell thee of.

Thus was Abraham inescapably confronted with his story problem, his equation: *piety + parental love = ?*

He was devout, pious, he loved the Lord. Aye, but also he loved his son, the only son he had. Caught on the merciless horns of a dilemma, it now seemed unavoidable that he must either disobey, and bring down upon himself the wrath of the Lord, or slay his own son.

He must somehow deal with that conflict by his own decision and action. For in his own breast, beyond all evasion, he had both love of the Lord and love of his son.

What did he decide and do?

He did precisely what you do when you solve $1+1=?$ in ordinary arithmetic.

He, like you in arithmetic, had been taught to keep the faith. He had been taught that when a choice must be made between obeying God or following the contrary directions of anyone or anything else, even one's own heart, the only "right" course is to obey God. He did what he had been taught was "right," with the same complete, unquestioning faith you show when you write a "2" after $1+1=$.

9

He obeyed the Lord. And then what happened?

He arrived at the "right," satisfying, unit answer, just as you do when you faithfully and correctly apply the principles of addition. Just before it was too late, there on the mountain, the Lord spoke again:

> And he said, Lay not thine hand upon the lad, neither do thou anything unto him: for now I know that thou fearest God, seeing thou hast not withheld thy son, thine only *son* from me.
>
> And Abraham lifted up his eyes, and looked, and behold behind *him* a ram caught in a thicket by his horns: and Abraham went and took the ram, and offered him up for a burnt offering in the stead of his son.

Abraham, that is, keeps both his son and his place in the Lord's affection. He leaves the mount of sacrifice with his two once apparently conflicting emotions added together, himself exalted by his God *and* his arms about his living son. Nor is even this all his reward, his "answer," for his supreme devotion to righteousness.

Still further, the Lord promises to multiply his seed, "as the stars of the heaven."

And the equation balances. For the supreme sacrifice, the supreme reward. For applying in blind, unquestioning faith the "right" principle, the "right" answer. And further, plainly this is a happy-ending, addition story; for as Abraham leaves the scene, has not his stature been added to? He is a bigger, greater character at the end than at the beginning.

Note now in passing that reasoning, as we have been taught to understand the term, does not enter into the solution of this problem at all. Abraham *does not* and *cannot* "reason" his way out of his dilemma, *he does not rationalize his problem.* He does what he *feels* is right. Story decisions and actions very seldom are based on reason. Almost always they are intuitive, just as here.

Whatever part human reason plays in real life (and there are those of us who maintain it is blessed little), in fiction it is far less important. Fiction is made of the bright, subjective fabric of dreams, of the stuff of that luminous world in which the impossible can happen, and does. And one's dreams—they are not of dead, dull facts and even deader reasoning,—rather they are almost pure emotion, darkened only by the thinnest film of that drab stuff, reality, which fills almost all our waking hours. This needs to be remembered. Feel, don't reason, your way through a story!

Now let us examine the $1 - 1 = ?$ formula.

Suppose we make it *love of god — love of worldly wisdom = ?* A problem of conditioned loves, in other words, sacred and profane. And once again, our equation probably suggests nothing to you—nothing at least until we clothe it with those real apples and people again. Or, rather, supply it with unclothed people, and apples and conditions quite too perfect to seem real. This is the formula of our Number One $1 - 1$ story, the tale of Adam and Eve.

It is Eve's story, obviously, *for these conflicting emotions must be in the same living breast, entertained simultaneously by one character.* And in this the problem is the same as that of the small boy who must learn to add or subtract 1 and 1 by himself.

You enhance and intensify the struggle by bringing in outside aids and allies on each side. That is, the serpent comes in to whisper to Eve to do the wrong thing, while Adam, presumably, exhorts her to do right. But you may not correctly place one of the contending emotions in the breast of one character and the other in another's.

Don't isolate your emotions so they can't fight. The

suspense of a short story comes almost altogether from the sensed struggle *inside the one principal character*. Will Eve listen to the wily serpent and eat of the tree of knowledge? Or will she obey the Lord and not eat? Place these antagonistic desires in the one arena of the character's breast, and make them fight!

All main characters in a correct story, incidentally, must each have his or her own particular internal struggle, else the characters never live. *Conflict creates character.* We shall go into this at length in the chapter on character. But at this point the first thing to realize is that, unless you intend writing a whole book, obviously you cannot follow in detail all the windings of all these different characters and their different conflicts.

You have to pick out one to emphasize while merely sketching in the others. Each of the characters has his own story, and you twist stories and characters together as you might the strands of a rope. But one strand is bright colored—the tale of the character you elect to follow.

You do not follow the strands of the other characters, *but they must cross your bright strand at the right places.* I mean, the bright strand of your hero, correctly twisted, must cross the dark strand of the villain at the precise spots where, if you were following the villain's strand instead, his dark trail would cross that of the hero. Else your whole story is weak, perhaps to failure. This is not so easy to grasp when it is briefly stated, as here. But we shall spend more time on it later. Meantime, watch it happen in our prime tale of Eve and the villain Snake.

The serpent whispers to her, and she is tempted, but at the same time is held back by fear of the Lord and his command. She is in suspense, story suspense. How else do you "suspend" anything save by pulling it two ways at the same time?

Dangle your watch on its chain—you pulling up, gravity down. Put your ring on a string and suspend it between your hands, one hand pulling right, the other left. Place Eve in suspension, with fear of the Lord pulling her one way, desire to yield to the serpent's temptings pulling the other. This is agonizing suspense.

Now what does Eve do?

She makes the "wrong," "sinful" decision and incarnates that decision in action. Just as Abraham proved his adherence to righteousness by obeying the Lord, binding Isaac, placing him on the altar, and raising the knife, so Eve demonstrates her submission to worldliness by eating the forbidden fruit. Further and worse, she gives some to Adam, and he eats, too. And what happens?

Here is swift subtraction.

First, there is laid upon them the curse of clothes, much more heavily upon the woman than upon the man. For, since she is the culprit, she deserves at least as much.

Next, they are deprived of the Garden of Eden and all the leisure that place connotes. Tossed out into the hard, pitiless world, to know cold and hunger and suffering, to have to work for a living, to have to fight thorns and bugs and thistles, to have to die. To know good and evil and have to choose between them. To possess the knowledge of God, but not the power . . .

That is punishment. Subtraction, swift, accurate, final. And note how each of the other characters also fulfills the story formula even while completing the tale of Eve.

The serpent, for his negative decision to tempt Eve, rather than be good and help her to be likewise—the serpent got his desserts, too, for his nefariousness. To crawl on his belly all the days of his life, to eat dust and be cursed above all cattle and every beast of the field, were his lot. While as for Mother Eve's gain, if any, that worldly knowledge . . .

$$1 - 1 = ?$$

Let us now set the two equations together, as we must in making all save the very simplest of stories. We shall have a $1+1=2$ for the deserving, virtuous hero or heroine and a $1-1=0$ for the villain. In the same story, mind you, and perhaps with the identical factors.

Thus in the parable of the Five Wise and the Five Foolish Virgins, the story equations are simply *urge for preparedness* + or − *love of ease*. The five wise virgins, following a plus equation, do the right thing: prepare their lamps beforehand, and so are permitted to greet the arriving bridegroom and enter and take their ease and pleasure at the wedding feast. But the five foolish virgins, adopting a minus equation, omit to provide themselves with the requisite wicks and oil. And so, for their answer, they get to howl, dance, and shiver in outer darkness.

The whole life of Christ as related in the Gospels is another example of intangible patterning: the supreme sacrifice to achieve the supreme reward—which is also the physicist's Third Law of Motion, "For every action an opposite and equal reaction." It is the Golden Rule—and good sportsmanship and the whole basis of the law upon which are erected our moralities and statutes and precepts for the conduct of the good life. No one can state such an eternal law as this in words that will fit everywhere, but one assuredly can catch the idea and apply it, nevertheless.

Incidentally, it might be noted in passing that the projection of the reward or answer into the future (as in the theological heaven for the righteous) is perfectly legitimate and permissible in fiction. Although preferably, for the benefit of the literal reader, you should reward your deserving hero here and, similarly, punish the villain here. To carry this aside still further, time, to a fictionist fictioneering, is something astoundingly different from time in its ordinary aspect. To a writer writing, time has no past or future, but only an eternal, all-inclusive *now*. But we shall look into all that in the next chapter; having planted the seed here, we may profitably go on with the plowing of other essential fields.

Remembering the thoroughly scientific, objective, doubt-worshipping school of education in which doubtless you were brought up, you may find the following commandment hard to live by. But mark it down as a vital necessity. *Do not approach your story problem in the scientific spirit of skepticism and doubt.*

I cannot emphasize this point too much. You simply must accept and believe first, that is, *have faith*, before you can produce *works*. Even your material scientist believes devoutly in doubt. You also, as a writer, must believe in something to begin with. You must believe in the validity of the moral principles you make your hero apply, in the solution of his problem, just as fervently and unquestioningly as you believe in the principles of arithmetic.

If faith without works is dead, why so equally are works, including fiction, without faith. You cannot, perhaps, merely make yourself believe, but you can write about problems whose solving principles you do accept. Do that!

And now, to confirm your faith in these simple formula patterns for short fiction, let us look at some of the formulas as employed in other people's stories, among them a number used by very famous fictionists.

Let us look first at one of the most perfect and deservedly famous short stories ever written, beloved Rober Louis Stevenson's *The Sire de Malétroit's Door:*

Immediately we discover formula, a simple one, too. Anyone who tells you the immortals of literature did not use formulas is misleading you. All three of Stevenson's principal characters follow the same basic equation. It is: *pride + love = ?*

Bare and unimaginative looking, isn't it? But look at what happens when this curt abstraction is clothed by the magic of Stevenson with the requisite apples and little Johnnies so that we may "see" it.

A proud, stiff-backed old gentleman, the *Sire de Malétroit* is exceedingly fond of his niece and ward, Blanche. Discovering that she is engaged in a surreptitious love affair, he sets a trap for her unknown gallant, into which falls:

Denis de Beaulieu, proud young cavalier and fighting man. Helplessly caught in the snare of Uncle's trick door and trusty men-at-arms, Denis is at once introduced to:

Blanche de Malétroit, the proud, beautiful young heroine. Regardless of their protests that they have never before seen each other, Uncle says cheerily that he thinks otherwise, and anyhow, no matter. He has tried to trap Blanche's young man for her. But now, either they may agree to wed or he proposes to hang Denis, *tout de suite.* The young couple may have two hours to decide what to do.

And there you are! *Pride + love = ?* in three incarnations, three versions, seemingly as different as day from night. Uncle's stiff family pride versus his love for his niece. Blanche's outraged feminine pride versus her love, if any, for a stranger, Denis. Denis's young male pride versus his love for Blanche, if any. It is a staggering, dramatic dilemma for both hero and heroine, particularly in the chivalrous nation and age in which the story is set.

What do they do? Regardless of whether you are acquainted with the story, you know instinctively and immediately what happens. They do the "right" thing, of course. Pride and honor and "I could not love thee, dear, so much, loved I not honor more"—these are all right in their place. But black dishonor is not involved here! It is merely pride versus love. And love rules the world. So, after almost two hours of being very proud at each other, the two youngsters realize they are in love, and each swallows his pride for the sake of the other. Chirping agreeably, the proud Sire de Malétroit lovingly greets his new nephew.

Pride + *love* = *pride and love combined in happiness.*

In Chapter VI you will find formulas of the short stories contained in assorted current magazines which chance to be on my desk as I write this. But if you cannot lay hand on these particular issues, no matter. Try the magazines available to you and see if you cannot write the formulas for at least three-fourths of the short fiction they contain. Many of these formulas will be transparently obvious.

Every magazine printing fiction, from the most bloodthirsty pulp to the most blue-blooded "quality" periodical, from the Sunday-school paper to the "true" detective magazine, buys formula, depends primarily on formula, satisfies its readers with formula. Let no one tell you otherwise.

Nor is there any fundamental difference in worth between the correctly done $1 + 1 = 2$, popular or pulp-type story and the $1 - 1 = 0$, "quality" story, so called. No more than there is between $1 + 1$ and $1 - 1$ in arithmetic. You need only ask anyone who says differently to explain why he considers it more vulgar to add than to subtract. Almost certainly you can show him that the tales of gloom and futility he prefers are simple $1 - 1$ affairs, and that his taste is so naïve it is shared by almost every college sophomore.

Nevertheless, before concluding this chapter with an inspection of some of these "quality" stories, perhaps we do need to concede that there is a strong tendency to assign different values, higher and lower "qualities," to the two equally valid, equally useful, elemental equations of our fictional mathematics. So much has been written about the art of writing that almost undoubtedly you will have read some of it, and having done so, you may be temporarily confused by the bald simplicities of which I speak here.

So far as I can determine, from a rather extensive reading of books on writing, this is the first one in which the basic, abstract patterns, or processes, of the short story have been completely separated and distinguished from the materials used to illustrate the problem.

Most writers, working by ear (and virtually all writers on writing, in my experience), are unable to separate their abstract "$1 + 1$" from the apples or oranges or heroines or villains—whatever they use to give flesh and blood to the equation. Accordingly, when writing on writing, these authors give you dissertations on how to illustrate one plus one with cocoanuts, instead of apples, or how to do it with apple pies.

They write, that is, about fashions rather than fundamentals. And while this may be very interesting, it is also quite incomprehensible, unless you, too, understand intuitively that they are not dealing primarily with cocoanuts or apple pies, but instead are trying to show that $1+1$, or *honor + love*, or *fear — greed*, or whatever the abstract equation may be, can be satisfactorily solved.

You may be experiencing this same difficulty in distinguishing between the arithmetical and the illustrative materials as you read this chapter. Forgive me if I seem to labor a point, but I cannot be too sure that I am clear. You may be asking yourself, for example, "Yes, but how can there be any such thing as an abstract emotion, *hate*, without *somebody to hate* and *something or somebody to be hated?*" Fair enough; how long did it take you to learn what "1" really meant in arithmetic?

You did not learn in a day, a week, or perhaps even a year that "1" did not necessarily mean an apple, or orange, or anything else real. And, perhaps, you believed for quite a while that there was one kind of "1" for the grocer, and another for the doctor, and still another for the policeman —it just must have been so, because they were such different people, with such different things and troubles to which to apply the concept of "1." But you think differently now.

Now, pointedly, there is no such thing as a "western equation," or a "love story" equation, or a "quality" equation—any more than there are different $1 + 1$ or $1 - 1$ equations for the grocer and the banker. Those who tell you otherwise are making the same primitive mistake the cavemen undoubtedly made when they first began to sense the abstract principles of addition, but were sure it could be done only with bearskins, or warclubs, or dinosaurs, or whatever else tangible they first saw incarnating the pattern.

Let us set up a so-called "quality" equation now and see with what utterly different materials and people we can make it real—for what vastly different markets we can shape it merely by changing the materials:

$$Pride - miserliness = ?$$

Make up your own story now, before you read another paragraph. Write it in brief synopsis. *Do it before you read a line more!*

#   #   #   #   #

All right, you have yours? Here is my story, done like yours, on the spur of the moment:

A rich, proud, and exceedingly avaricious banker has a young wife whom he treats in niggardly fashion, buying all her clothes for her, allowing her no spending money, even refusing to permit her to have charge accounts. In fact, just the day before our story opens, the miserly wight has flatly refused her a badly needed, very becoming, yes, a modestly priced gown she has seen in the window of a downtown shop.

At noon the banker intends to bid in a certain Indian-land mineral lease being offered at auction by the government. He has private information of a very valuable lead and zinc deposit on this land. (He has obtained this information from a poor debtor who came to the house several nights before, pleading for an extension of his mortgage. In return for the information, the banker promised him this, but after the poor fellow had left, laughingly pointed out to his wife that the promise was not in writing, nor did the debtor have any witnesses, since a wife cannot testify against her husband.) The banker expects to get the lease at a tithe its true value and he fears only one other possible bidder, a bumptious (as the banker deems him) geologist who has endeared himself to Mrs. Banker by chaffing the financial magnate about his stinginess and, even worse, sympathizing with the young wife.

Just before the auction begins, a talebearer comes rushing to inform the banker that the geologist and the banker's wife are downtown at the dress shop, where the geologist is buying the gown for the wife. This, incidentally, is edifying several of the local society dowagers who are eavesdropping. In a frothing fury of outraged pride, the banker snarls at his secretary to bid for him and rushes downtown to the dress shop.

His wife and the geologist are gone. But, yes, says the gossipy manager, he certainly did buy the gown for Mrs. Banker, had her try it on and wear it, and they went off together. Mad enough to bite nails, the banker searches vainly, at last remembers the auction, and rushes back to encounter his dismayed henchman, the secretary.

"I tried to remind you that you have to bid in person and present the cash with your bid," the secretary wails. "You hung onto the money when you ran off. The geologist bid in the lease. But he left you this letter."

The letter (haven't you guessed it by now!) reads:

"Figured you'd leave the field to me when I sent that guy to tell you what I was doing. Your wife gets the dress for telling me about the zinc deposit. When she gets back from Reno, she and I are going to get the money the lease will bring. And you, Skinflint, for pinching your pennies, this is what you get."

#　#　#　#　#

Have you noticed how lovingly, and with entirely too many words, I adorn even the skeleton of my child? A poor child, perhaps, but my own. Now let us see what a great master of quality fiction, Guy de Maupassant, did with an identical equation. Where I do pulp, he accomplished literature. Like this:

In his immortal *The Piece of String*, the central character, the miserly yet very proud Maître Hauchecorne, picks up a worthless bit of string and is seen doing it. Shamed, he makes matters worse by immediately hiding the string, trying to camouflage his action.

When, later, he is accused of having picked up and kept a lost pocketbook, he tells the truth about his little exhibition of miserliness and pride. But now nobody will believe him. Not even when the purse is found will people concede his honesty. And so, overwhelmed by the world's insistance on believing the worst, he dies of a broken heart.

Pride — miserliness . . . $1 - 1 = ?$

II

Viewpoint: Space and Time

Unto you it is given to know the mysteries . . . but
to others in parables; that seeing they might not
see, and hearing they might not understand.

LUKE, 8:10

WITH a story, as with a woman, we are too apt to
overlook the first fundamental. But mark it down!
No matter how perfectly formed, how gifted, ingenious,
and developed and adorned, all these mean nothing if the
subject is not first alive. Into your creature of words or
clay you must somehow contrive to breathe the breath of
life. Else all your labor is in vain.

And I come now to another something so very simple
it is very, very difficult.

It will help here, although it is by no means necessary,
that you know something of religion.

I do not mean religion in the academic sense. Nor am I
even referring to formal adherence to any particular de-
nomination. I mean, if at any time in your life you have
experienced that spiritual feeling which defies any satisfactory defining, then you are going to have a considerably easier time grasping what follows. But even if you
have never felt the spirit, do not despair. It still can happen, you know, to anybody, anywhere.

Not only can it happen, but it may have special significance for the writer. For those who write fiction are a
variety of lay priests. They are not actually permitted to
preach, but they do furnish the parables confirming the

22

moralities taught by the clergy. Further, there is an unmistakably biblical flavor in the writer's whole procedure, creating, as he does, out of the void; making a world, not as it is, but as he feels it should be; peopling it with creatures, also of his making; governing them with inexorable laws; rewarding them for righteousness; punishing them for wrong doing. He himself stands supreme, above all space and time. And, most mysterious of all, he somehow brings all of this process of creation to life.

How does he do it?

He does it primarily by using a fictional viewpoint, *a particular way of looking at his story problems and materials.*

He sees things ordinary people do not. His wisdom most assuredly is not of this world—almost anyone who has known fiction writers will confirm this. He has something of the genuine prophet's gift of foresight—and this is no idle fancy, not even scientifically speaking. He has, perhaps, extra sensory perception, the weird but apparently well-founded ability of some people to see the shape of things to come, events before they happen. And finally, much more like an immortal than a mere human, the fiction writer is limited, in his stories at least, by no past or future but lives in an eternal *now*.

Let us see how he does all this—and, for both our sakes, I hope it can be done by means less drastic than those once used on a sturdy sinner named Saul on the road to Damascus. If the blinding flash comes only as a gentle glow, it will at least be easier on the eyes.

He does it by looking at his world subjectively, rather than objectively.

True creative art is nothing more than the application of this very simple and natural way of *seeing from the subjective side of the artist to the subjective side of that with which he deals.* Although one could be very profound about this, pointing out, for example, that it is the essence of the first of the six great canons of art laid down in sixth century China, still there is no good reason whatever for saying it in Chinese.

Everyone knows what I mean. Everyone, even the objective scientist, uses subjective vision every day of his life.

A bug, sitting on the back of a moving truck, sees only telephone poles, road signs, cross streets, buildings, and so on—all kinds of objects rushing crazily to the rear. That is objective vision. Seeing thus, he perceives by his vague bug intelligence that there assuredly is no purpose or meaning whatever to all of the mad, backward rush of objects into history. Nor can he do anything at all about it, except, perhaps classify the objects, assign a Latin name to each pole as it passes, and thus prove himself a true scientist.

The pole that kills him, however (if the truck chances to run into a pole), will remain as nameless as it was unexpected. Nor will all his objective science save him, since he can't see when to duck.

But how about the driver of the truck?

He is not looking backward—he looks *forward*. He *knows* the actual movement is not of poles and signs and other objects backward, into scientific classification and history, but, instead, of himself and his vehicle forward. He is not helpless against the seeming rush of objects, as is the bug in rear—he can *do* something about the poles and other objects; he can at least dodge them, steer for himself a safe course. *He is looking from his subjective side, his advancing front, to the front, the subjective side, of all those things coming at him.* And so, to a degree at least, he is the captain of his soul and the master of his fate.

Why? Because he is part of *that which moves.* Because, looking ahead, he can and does act, *continuously, now*, to avoid foreseen, subjective, but not yet accomplished and so objectified, collisions, scrapes, troubles. Nor does he need any book, any scientific classifications giving the exact names and genera of all those not-yet-objective things, in order to avoid them. On the contrary, if he had to stop and look in the book each time . . .

Further, he can and does prolong his subjective, looking-ahead vision, perhaps far, far beyond the objectively visible horizon. He knows where he is going, that truckdriver. He can visualize his goal. So he shapes his course accordingly, even though he cannot "really" see the place as yet; and thus he gives a pattern and purpose and meaning to his way. Moreover, as he moves, the world, to him, becomes more and more the precise opposite of what it seems to the objective visioned bug in rear.

The longer the journey, the greater the dismaying disintegration of the world from the bug's viewpoint. More and more and more meaningless things, a torrent of them! But to the driver—one less block, one less crossroad, one less river to cross! Fewer and fewer the things of this world ahead and all of them leading him home, until at last he is rolling the final yard to his goal, *one place!*

Project this subjective vision one step further, over the last horizon, and you have the religious concept, the pure subjective. Extend the bug's vision far enough backward and you have the pure objective. Here we are concerned with neither extreme. So I need only point out the practical and immediate connotations.

Fiction, like any other virile reality in this world, is both objective and subjective, both tangible thing and intangible driving force. But primarily and fundamentally it is a force, driven forward by a sentient creator, the writer, over a foreseen path to a foreseen goal. And please note foresight is the opposite of hindsight! Whenever a given piece of work does not meet these requisites, when it does not move under its own power, when it is not under control, when it does not, as it were, march to the beat of unstruck, unheard but certain music, through unwritten yet sure measures to an inevitable goal—when it is more objective than subjective, more fact than fiction—then it is not fiction.

And this, to be sure, is so simple it is exceedingly hard to see; particularly when one has been bred (as who nowadays has not) in the hard, too-materialistic, too-objective, too-scholastic world of modern education. Yet let me try to say it even more simply.

You take a piece of steak on your plate. The steak is a tangible thing, there on the plate, an object. It has all the objective aspects, shape, size, form, color, feel, perhaps even sound, an appetizing sizzle. But in all of that it is, as yet, no good whatever to you.

You must first eat it, digest it—a process, incidentally, requiring no conscious thought—before you may make use of its goodness. Only when it has lost all form, shape, size, color, mass, and every other aspect which you identify as objectively "real," only then can you actually put it to use. But when at last it is energy in your system, when it has been transformed from a "what" into a "how" —then, perhaps, you make use of that energy to write a story, fix a clock, invent something, or do something else worth possibly a hundred times as much as the steak. And how did you accomplish this?

By precisely the same general pattern that was applied when you mastered every skill or art you own, whether it be swimming, bicycle riding, shooting, painting, the use of fine tools, generalship, salesmanship, and so on. You began with the stomach for it; the ability to digest—a something, be it noted, you did not consciously acquire. Next, consciously, you gathered the objective materials, the textbook, the swimming instructor, the bicycle, the

26

paint brushes. You struggled with them, more or less maddened by the hard, alien objectiveness of the things, by their stubborn refusal to be and to do as you wished. Perhaps, time and again, you almost gave up.

And then something happened. At last digestion began. At last those stubborn objectionables began to melt; the frozen "what's" began to thaw, to change to fluid "how's"; at long last, with a rush of joy, you knew that you knew! No need now to try to remember the book, the rules, the instruction. No need to stop and take thought. Now you knew and could do. And in some measure, in that instant, you had linked hands with eternity.

None is ever so humble as to have no skill at all; none has failed to do something, to know sometime that joyous thrill. It is that simple! From the baby, crowing in the sunlight as for the first time he touches his own toes, to us, to the great mathematician so unscientifically crying "Eureka!" as he makes his find, to the master artist, painting at last with the tip of his very soul for brush, the secret is shared by us all.

"What" into "how!" It is the secret of all wisdom.

Yet potent also is that other power which we may not control, the creeping paralysis of the objective. Face it, gaze overlong into that abyss, and presently, as mad Nietzsche said, you will find the abyss gazing also into you. Before its stare you freeze as helpless and enchanted as a bird before a great snake. How, then, do you break the charm?

You break it by turning your back. By looking the other way.

Look at this single word for illustration, pro and con:

OBJECT

It is an object, is it not? It is a word. Yes, but further, in that aspect, *it is in your past.*

Consciously or otherwise, you know it required a space of time for the light to leap from the word to your eye, and still more time for your eye to receive and translate the message, for the tidings to travel up the optic nerves, for the brain to receive and act on the message. Perhaps it was indeed a very small space of time. But no matter. In that small time the word changed subtly, and that ineffable Whatever-It-Is inside you there, that ego, that "Me" traveled on. Thus, in effect, already going away from the word, you looked back and saw it not as it is, but as it was. Precisely as, at night, you look up at a great star, seeing it not as it is now, but instead as it was, perhaps thousands of years ago when the light reaching you now first started from that star; perhaps also even with that "tail-light" effect astronomers have observed, that shift to the red, that going away appearance which has led many to believe the universe is expanding. It happens also in the minute space between you and the word.

And there is more. You know you cannot change your past. Though, undoubtedly, it can and does change you.

You cannot even go back and un-read that one word. Object! Subtly it has changed you forever, leaving at least its tiny mark. It cannot be erased now.

> *The Moving Finger Writes, and having Writ*
> *Moves on, nor all thy Piety nor Wit*
> *Shall lure it back to cancel half a Line*
> *Nor all thy Tears wash out a Word of it.*

And that is objective reality; and if that is all you can see, if that is your only way, then indeed you are lost.

Yet there must be a front, as well as a back, to anything real, and always the front must face in the opposite direction from the back. Which is a simplicity that quite escapes too many of the learned. The bug on the back of the truck, old Aesop's flea riding the chariot axle, cries out, "See, see what a great dust I am raising!" But the driver, who knows, is looking the other way.

A mere word, an object, destroys reality? We may change it thus:

I OBJECT!

And thus, by changing the direction of view, by giving priority to life, I have done something profound. Let me now apply it directly to the art of writing, with pictures and examples:

In the bug's-eye manner of objective writing you were taught to work from right to left, as it were. Most painfully and unnaturally you learned to eliminate, as far as possible, all subjective aspects and, instead, to describe succinctly just how the object or action "looked to you."

But "to," please note, means "toward." That is, precisely as science taught you about the light waves, namely that they came from the object to your eye, so in writing you were taught to set the source of enlightenment, the viewpoint, in the dead object and have it look toward you. Like this:

ME ← ← ← OBJECT

This assuredly would eliminate any emotion, interest, natural understanding, or other subjective quality that the living "Me" might see in the object. The fallacy of it was detected long ago by Immanuel Kant, the philosopher, who considered all space subjective, and held also that viewpoint is the ultimate essential reality, giving shape and significance to all else. But the result of this process of letting the dead object look and talk is scientific writing. Like this:

"The specimen undoubtedly was *M. mephitis*, although it was scrawny and poorly marked. There was evidence of parasitic infestation and pathologic degeneration of the vegetal functions. Atrophy of the renal glands was particularly marked. The sacroiliac . . ."

But enough. Observe, if you please, how little alive is *M. mephitis*.

Now let us reverse this objective (which is another term for dead) topic and write it subjectively, looking from the living side of the writer to the living side of the animal considered—a polecat, in plain, subjective language. We shall write now like this:

ME $\rightarrow$ $\rightarrow$ $\rightarrow$ OBJECT

"I discovered the old fellow living under my cabin floor, and with a due regard for western proprieties, plus a horrid suspicion of what he is, I have let him severely alone. Apparently he is one of the old settlers around these parts, for he is as gaunt as western settlers are; and I fear also is afflicted with fleas. Most of the time, too, he seems very crabbed and dyspeptic, embittered, I suppose, about the passing of free grass and the open range. And it may be he has his opinions of city dudes and such, now all too frequent in God's country. But I must admit, thus far he has been a civil civet and there has not been the faintest hint of a neighborhood smell. Perhaps he is too old. But the other night, regardless, I saw him playing in the moonlight, solemnly chasing his tail, behaving for all the world like a slightly rheumatic kitten. I was tempted to toss him a spool. How this will come out . . ."

Note how unmistakably the one way of writing reverses the other. Whereas the objective paragraph refers beyond doubt to the past, kills the polekitty, dissects him, gets right down to the dead, objective, outside of every detail, the subjective paragraph does just the reverse.

Each paragraph tells the same facts, that the animal was aged, gaunt, flea infested, not in the best of health, etc. But, plainly, the subjective paragraph's time is now, the direction of its gaze toward the future. It does not kill the polecat. It lets him live. It records virtually everything in terms of "I" and "me." "I discovered." "I saw." "I was tempted." It does not analyze and explain, it arouses and stimulates instead. And—most important of all to grasp— it does this by reversing the usual relationship of subject and object. Instead of letting the object look "to" the subject, the ego, the living "Me," that "Me" looks at the object.

If this technique takes time to master, do not despair. Solemnly teaching you through the years to suppress or deny the subjective, science has conveniently ignored its own plain dictum, "For every action, an equal and opposite reaction," nor has it deigned to explain, what, then, goes back from the observer to the observed while the observer is busy describing how the observed "looks to" him? But here are some simple rules of thumb to help you guide your work and judge it when you have finished:

(1) There must always be at least one living viewpoint in a story, one character whom you and the reader alike feel vividly to be in the actual first person.

Now take warning! This is that tricky reversal. The idea is so to describe and handle this one character that any reader, anytime, anywhere, will feel, immediately and unmistakably, "Why, this is my own story, all about me!"

And you get this effect by yourself, as writer, thinking in the first person about this viewpoint character. Think, "This is me!"

You may, indeed, write about this viewpoint character in the grammatical third person. That is, you may use "he," "his," and even his name to identify him, rather than employ the confession story style, "I," "me," "my." But do not let this formality confuse you.

Remember, in a fact story, for example, an ordinary news account in your newspaper, the power originates in the action, event, or person observed. It runs from right to left, from the thing reported to the reporter. And the reporter simply leaves himself out; or, rather, tries to. But in a fiction story, using perhaps the same third-person diction, you, the fictionist, do just the reverse.

You put yourself in. You imagine yourself clear inside the viewpoint character's brain, seeing with his eyes, hearing through his ears, feeling with his body, privy to his most secret thoughts. And you tell those thoughts.

You cannot see the viewpoint character's face, please note. You're inside! He's you, for the time being. You can't see the back of your own head, or the angry gleam in your own eyes, or the delicate flush on your own cheeks. Accordingly, when describing the viewpoint character, do not put such objective aspects in. But you can feel your own emotions, can't you, even the most private ones? Put these in, all of them!

An objective news reporter is commanded never to color the news, never to put in his own emotions, what he felt about it all. Very well, you do just the opposite. You put in nothing that is not colored by your emotions. And *never* make objective things of those emotions. Instead, imagine them as colored glasses through which (not at which) you look to get the desired effect.

Thus, to describe anger on the part of your viewpoint character (or VP, in writer's jargon), you just see red, maybe like this:

"A swift crimson smoke came whirling across my vision, and I could feel the angry heat in my cheeks as I turned."

Note how plainly the descriptions are from the inside of the VP character looking outward. And now note also how this unmistakable direction is not changed at all when I change the sentence to third person:

"A swift crimson smoke came whirling across his vision, and he could feel the angry heat in his cheeks as he turned."

So much for that.

(2) All other characters in your story, being essentially objects outside the VP character, must be described objectively, that is, just as you ordinarily see somebody else.

For example, to record that same emotion, anger, but this time on the part of a character other than the VP character:

"He flushed angrily, and I could see the swift red flecks in his narrowed eyes."

Plainly, that is "Me" looking at "him," isn't it? I see his outward physical changes, which I interpret as anger on his part. And it is equally plain that "he" is not the VP character. The VP could not see his own angry flush, "red flecks in narrowed eyes," etc. But now let us change the VP to third person again, calling the "I" by a given name, "Sam."

"He flushed angrily, and Sam could see the swift red flecks in his narrowed eyes."

Obviously, this does not change the direction or the unmistakable identity of the VP in the least.

(3) The running time of the story, as you write (or read) it, must always be the immediate present, now, *the only time in which life exists.*

This, again, is reversal. You write in the past tense, but you must always think in the present, looking to the future. Always, you must think of the VP character as yourself, *right this instant.* And this means, among other things, that you cannot stop and record matters that have hap-

33

pened in the story past unless the VP character quite naturally and logically is remembering them now. And what you are writing about is the VP remembering them now and *not* primarily the past events themselves.

(4) Your emotions, not your facts, are the power of your story.

This is actually just another way of saying, "Write subjectively, use VP, color everything." But here, specifically, it means, give power to the story by beginning more than half of your sentences with unmistakable recordings from that living, emotionalizing "Me," "right now," VP. Thus:

"I was tempted." "Angrily, I whirled." "A dry despair gnawing through my (or his) brain, I (or he) waited." "Clenching his fists he waited, saw his chance and leaped." And so on.

Incidentally, this is also the prime test of whether any piece of writing is fictional or factual. Looking backwards most of the time, the factual writer simply records the dead facts, with little or no indication of the emotional response on the part of the passive "Me." Logically, he puts his topic of first importance—those dead facts—first. He writes, "This specimen was . . ." "It was scrawny." "There were evidences of . . ." And so on.

Looking forward, the fiction writer reverses this, putting his topics of first importance—his emotions and actions—first. "I felt . . ." "I was tempted . . ." "Angrily, I whirled . . ."

Frequently, though not always, you can take a page of good fiction, containing, say, a dozen sentences, and discover that about seven or eight of the sentences begin as above. A page of factual writing will reveal just the reverse, or worse.

(5) Make no real breaks between paragraphs.

Formal writing, because it is based on the material way of looking backward at reality—that is, on looking at and analyzing dead objects—dissects the topic, neatly separating each sub-topic into a separate paragraph, with a noticeable break between paragraphs. But . . . there are no breaks in the thread of life.

Obviously, if a break does occur, it is just there that life ends. Accordingly, in fiction writing, you write what looks like a formal paragraph but actually is not.

Each paragraph will "hook" into the next without any real break. What ordinarily would be the first sentence of the next paragraph will be set as the last sentence of the paragraph in hand. Or a question calling for an answer will end the paragraph, with the expected answer, of course, coming up immediately in the next paragraph. This is called the paragraph hook.

(6) It is permissible to change viewpoints in a story, but only when you change cleanly from one individual viewpoint to another and notify your reader immediately of the change.

You cannot have omniscient VP in a correct story, or, that is, the viewpoint of God, knowing everything, past, present and future, everybody's secret thoughts, feelings, actions and intentions, all at the same time. You must confine yourself to one VP at a time, remembering that not even the famous general actually got on his horse and rode off in all directions at once.

But you can change VP's in a single story, just as you can change trains in a single journey. Do it just as you would change trains. That is, (a) get off your original VP train; (b) walk across the station platform, which is usually a white-space break between the sections of your story; (c) get on your new VP train and let your reader know immediately he is now riding a different VP. For illustration, this:

A bitter tumult of emotions in his brain, Don Dashaway stared at the little Captain for a long moment, then turned reluctantly away. After all, the little Captain was of age. And then some! If he wanted to play the fool, there was nothing Don Dashaway could do about it.

But any wish to play the fool was far from the little Captain's mind as he watched Dashaway's broad back merge into the scurrying crowd. That Don figured he was at least getting senile, that this was going to make him look like an idiot—at least until the scheme worked —the Captain knew very well. But, stubbornly, the Captain was just not going to let any mere pride and appearance balk him in doing what he considered right.

Ah, that's enough. Note how the first paragraph unmistakably is from Don Dashaway's VP, placing "Me" in Dashaway's brain, the only place where "Me" could be standing in order to know Dashaway's inner emotions and thoughts. Further, the other character, the Captain, is described as "Me" would see him, from inside Dashaway's brain.

But, after the "change-trains" break, notifying the reader that something is happening, it is easy to observe how the reader is immediately informed that the VP is now in another brain, that of the Captain.

"Me," looking through the Captain's eyes, sees Dashaway's receding back, an obvious impossibility from Dashaway's VP. "Me" now is privy to the Captain's secret thoughts and feelings, although these are still mysteries to Dashaway—although they would still be mysteries to "Me" as well, had not the VP been shifted to the Captain's mind. Make your VP changes in this general manner.

But as a friendly caution, I suggest that you will do well to master the telling of a story from one VP first, before you tackle the more complex matter of multiple viewpoint. Single VP stories can be and are sold to all markets, including the best. And you will recall that you learned simple arithmetic before undertaking complex fractions and quadratics.

(7) Make your transitions on a continuing stream of emotion.

Let us suppose that we wish our VP character to leap a dead interval of time or space or both, an interval we have to have in the story, but in which nothing particularly dramatic or interesting happens. We can do it. In the fictionist's jargon this is called a *transition*. You must accomplish many of them, both great and small, in almost all stories.

You do it simply by continuing the living quality, the emotion, across the gap, meanwhile blithely leaving out all the continuity of small incidents, the eye blinkings, the breathings, the countless other dull, physical, objective things the character must have gone through to cover the dropped space and time. It is easily done.

Perhaps it may amaze you to realize (as you will, on thinking about it) that never have you seen real movement in any movie you ever attended. That is, unless the film broke in the machine. All you saw was a series of motionless pictures, with the movements of shining celluloid shadows made only in the projection machine, while the screen itself was dark! Yet, so powerful is the imagination that you came home with a very good idea of what happened and what the characters did! Very well, make use of that powerful imagination, in your reader, as well as in yourself!

At the beginning of the transition, emphasize the emotion, the strong upward lift of the VP character's feeling. Then, if the area of time or space you are dropping is at all sizeable, put in a white space to denote as much. Then, as you begin again on the other side of the gap, emphasize the

emotion once more, making it unmistakable to the reader
that the living thread of the story has successfully crossed
the chasm.

To illustrate, we may pick up our Don Dashaway
from the example just given on how to make viewpoint
changes, and, instead of changing to the little Captain's
VP, simply move Don through a transition, say, two days
and one hundred miles.

> A bitter tumult of emotions in his brain, Don Dash-
> away stared at the little Captain for a long moment,
> then turned reluctantly away. After all, the little Cap-
> tain was of age. And then some! If he wanted to play
> the fool, there was nothing Don Dashaway could do
> about it.

> But the worry and the maddening sense of foolish-
> ness of it all still rode with him, nevertheless, as Don
> arrived home two days later. Two days and one hun-
> dred slow miles of thinking hadn't changed a thing,
> hadn't brought a single gleam of light. What on earth
> a man should do about such a stubborn old fool . . .

The points to note are these: this time we did not
change trains, from Don's VP to the Captain's. This time
we continued in Don's VP. And, obviously, something
has carried the story across that blank interval—that three
space break—just as though it were not there.

That something is the continuing emotion, Don's
worry and feeling of futility. Just as we leave him on the
other side of the gap, he is very busy worrying and feeling
helpless. And on this side of the transition, he is *still* wor-
ried and feeling baffled, "two days later," and "one hundred slow miles" away. So casually are these latter two
dead, objective facts introduced that we scarcely notice
them. Yet we have dropped out of our account a huge
area of space and time, two days and one hundred miles.

It does not bother the reader at all. Why? Because he has imagination too. We told him the important part, that there was no break in the important part, in the living stream of the story, in Don's worry. That did not even change. The story flows on, unbroken, and the reader supplies the objective lack. Do you get the idea?

These seven points are about all the elements of viewpoint you need to master, although, naturally, the topic is capable of almost infinite elaboration. Recognition of this one great way of breathing life into your words is by no means original with me, incidentally. All successful fiction writers employ VP in some one of its variations, usually by ear, as it were; and how true it is that one who sees through his ears sometimes sees darkly. But further, in one way or another, nearly all the great religions and philosophical thinkers, pagan as well as Christian, express the same fruitful idea.

"There is nothing that is not objective; there is nothing that is not subjective," wrote Chuang Tsu, the great Chinese mystic of the fourth century before Christ. And now follow him: "But it is impossible to start from the objective. Only from subjective knowledge is it possible to proceed to objective knowledge. The true sage . . . places himself in subjective relation with all things."

Which is just what I have been trying to explain. And now, in the contrariwise fashion of the Western world, let us try to analyze this strange phenomenon of subjective relationship, or viewpoint, objectively:

If you will ponder it, you will see quite plainly that this subjective relationship between you, the writer, and your story is an amalgamation of three entities. It is a trinity, strongly reminiscent of the religious Trinity. And quite understandably so, too, since these, our stories, are a mimic world into which we propose to breathe both spirit and life. It is, by parts, (1) the author, (2) the VP character and (3) the reader.

(1) The author, like God to the greater, real world, stands as lord, master, and creator to the tiny world of his story. The author knows all, sees all, is not bound by time, space, or circumstance, and guides his creatures just as the real Creator guides us—by the still, small, inaudible voice of conscience.

(2) The VP character, like the Son in the theological Trinity, is the visible "Me." He knows only what he has seen, heard, felt, tasted, and touched in his past, plus—and be it not ignored!—that different wisdom within, that whispering by the still, small voice of the ineffable truths. By this inner voice he is linked to his author, as we to ours. Like us, he cannot always be sure of this voice. Like us, he must grapple constantly with the problems of the present, and no more than we can he see the future. Like us, he lives only in the present, *remembering* back and *hoping* or *fearing* ahead.

(3) The reader is that mysterious third member of the trinity, the Holy Ghost, of whom we have only the vaguest conception. But in fiction, at any rate, we know that he associates and identifies himself with principally the Son, the VP character. This is why, as prudent writers, we refrain from giving too many outward physical details of our VP character. How do we know what the reader looks like?

And now we are set up to try to understand this VP trinity in action, to watch it clothe a cold plot equation with warmth, life, and action. Here is how a story is conceived, plotted, and written:

(1) The creator, or author, poses the plot.

Fundamentally, he does this, as we have already noted in Chapter I, by setting up a seeming dilemma with which to try his characters.

"What would I do if I were Abraham, torn between love of my son and fervent desire to obey the Lord?"

"What would I do were I Eve, struggling between a wish to eat of the tree of knowledge and an almost equally strong contrariwise impulse to obey my Creator?"

(2) The author creates a character to struggle with the problem.

This central character may or may not be the VP character. Ordinarily and most simply he is. But sometimes a comparatively minor character is used, to sit and watch the struggle—life and drama from a ringside seat, so to speak. Quite often in the past, but more rarely today, this spectator VP character is the author himself. But about this it is well to remember that, although in ancient days, the gods did come down to earth now and then, in these days they save themselves much possible embarrassment and trouble by staying away.

It is, I mean, best practice just now to make the VP character one of the fictional people in the story, preferably the hero or heroine.

(3) The character then struggles with and solves the problem.

And you, the author, in writing of his struggles, do a quick change from primarily the creator to primarily that VP character. You *are* that living person for the time being; and you let him feel nothing, think nothing, do nothing you cannot vividly imagine yourself thinking, feeling, or doing under the given circumstances.

I mean—and take this literally—you laugh, cry, hope, despair, rage, and rejoice with him. For if you cannot feel to the fullest degree with your character, you cannot make him come fully to life. So lock yourself up in a private cell, if you think you must, but do not hesitate to laugh, cry real tears, get furiously angry, or whatever, as your character meets situations evoking these emotions.

For when you do, you will find a very strange and cheering thing beginning to happen.

The words you write will begin to be charged with story vitality. They may look just the same as before. A dead automobile battery usually looks just the same as a live one, too. But hooked up, both the charged story word and the live auto battery promptly produce the kick that makes all the difference in the world. Being the VP character, having emotions with him, is the way you put in that kick.

Secondarily, of course, all through this procedure of being primarily the VP character you remain also the creator. As the creator, you help the VP character to "see" his problem. You do this just as the real Creator in real life does it for us, by introducing the proper materials, people, and circumstances at the proper time—just as the first-grade teacher puts the apples on the desk at the proper time for the six-year-old to see, and then guides him more or less subtly in his struggles to make $1+1=2$.

Yours, naturally, is a somewhat harder task than that of your primary teacher, since your must create the apples also. You must play two conflicting emotions against each other, constantly reinforcing each side until the final showdown is reached. You must bring in villains to fight on the side of evil, saints to preserve us in the paths of righteousness. You stage a more or less gaudy outer struggle. *But the primary struggle,* never forget, *remains in the one central character's breast.*

Like conscience, you whisper into the character's ear that understandably "right" thing to do, while at the same time making it just as hard as possible for him to do it, of course. And then, when he does it, you, the creator, have his reward prepared and ready.

Simply because he chooses the "right" course, you, the creator, let him arrive at the right destination, his reward.

And I mean this in precisely the same way that you, traveling a strange highway and coming to a fork in the road, would take the right course if someone you trusted implicitly had told you that was the way to your desired destination.

I am speaking here principally of a plus-equation story. In a minus equation you do the same in reverse: bring your character up to his decision, let him make the "wrong" choice, and so arrive at his punishment. Just how it may be in the real scheme of things, I do not know and offer no conjectures, but in fiction at least we are pretty fatalistic; and a "good" ending or a "bad" one is planned and ordained from the beginning. Poor characters, perhaps it's just as well they're only paper creations after all!

(4) The reader, the third part of the subjective trinity, simply hitch hikes on the VP character, vicariously experiencing with him whatever may befall him. Or, if the VP character is not the central character, the reader enjoys himself at third hand—which perhaps explains why minor character VP's are not too popular in popular type magazines. Principally, you keep your "Holy Ghost" component in mind only to slant and condition your story for its potential market.

Thus, very seldom do you address a story to "everybody," for if you do you will ordinarily fail to please anybody. Instead, you narrow your audience to some one of the literary-taste groups. You try to imagine the likes and dislikes of one of those truly imponderable people, a typical *Saturday Evening Post* reader, or *Collier's* fan, or *Atlantic Monthly*, or *Woman's Home Companion*, or *Wild West Weekly* buyer. And then you try to fit your plot problem, your characters, language, and especially your action and reward, or punishment, to that ghostly consumer of your wares.

You represent the consumer, too, remember, as you

write. Even if he is a ghost, do try to give the poor fellow better representation than he usually receives in the councils of management, labor, and consumers. You will receive your reward, if nowhere else, in heaven.

Do I need to observe now that, although that which I have described is the formal procedure you go through in plotting and writing a story, it is not necessarily the only way you can do it?

Most businesses operate on much the same pattern, considering capital and management first (and most of the rest of the time as well), labor next, and the consumer last of all. But they do not always do that—not even the highly successful businesses. In reaching for your story, you, just as any other business enterprise, may come first upon any part of it, supplying the other parts later.

You may see only the plot problem first, and then need to create or discover the characters, circumstances, etc., to incarnate it. Or you may see the principal character (this seems to be the most common procedure, especially for beginning writers), and then have to create a problem to fit. Or you may see first only the opening situation, with no characters or problem clear enough to formulate, or the end, the answer, or even the middle.

It does not matter. Knowing what you are expected to do, knowing the parts and pattern, you can readily supply the missing pieces, working backwards, forwards, or even both ways from the middle.

Finally, of course, you may be merely a would-be author in search of everything. In that case I commend you to the mercies of the Lord.

Intimately associated with the matter of VP are the problems of space and time, which we had already begun to touch upon earlier in this book. (And, incidentally, since this is a subjective book, you will find it returning again and again to the same subject, saying the same thing in different ways, trying, at least, to achieve a unity and a singleness that is just the opposite of the objective dissection you have learned to expect in non-fiction books.) Now we look at our story business from another angle, that of time–space.

Already we have noted that the writer, like the Lord, is not bound by space or time, though the character is, alas. So here we are up against something not as simple as might be wished for.

But neither is it too complex—at least not in fiction. Like a character in real life, your fiction character lives only in the present, in the *right now*. Thus, whether you use the past tense, as most writers do, or something else, you, the writer, need only remember that necessity and feel that the time is *now* in every sentence you write, as you write it. Whereupon, if you have done it even ordinarily well, that obliging ghost, the reader, will also feel, *this is right now*, whenever and wherever his eye chances to alight upon your lines. And you have won half your battle to make that reader feel your story is alive.

But you do have to remember that the ineffable *now* goes with the reader's glance. As he reads on through your story, the "*now*" and the life of your character both follow his reading eye. That is fine. But if that reader shifts his glance, his attention, "*now*" still goes with that glance. The character and your story momentarily are deserted and dead. Perhaps you and the reader can resurrect them, perhaps not. You, the author, must try your best to avoid this dangerous situation and so write your story that the reader cannot stop reading, not even for an instant.

That, I have to concede, is an ideal and a perfection you may practically never attain. But you will try for it, nevertheless. And you will help yourself by knowing something about story time and space and how to use them so that they will not tire your reader—so that he actually is not conscious either of the space of time he consumes in reading, or of the fatigue and dullness of the story years and distances you must work into your fiction.

The idea, I mean, is to make the reader spellbound and keep him that way.

Very well. Now, as the author, you have to grasp the truth that you have a wholly different kind of time and space that your character, or even your reader. For, to you, the whole space of the story must be one continuous *now*. You have to write it that way, going over and over it, backwards and forwards if necessary, until no matter where a reading eye chances to alight, the spot is *right now* and the life flows forward from that spot—just as your eye and attention follow these lines.

"The Moving Finger writes; and, having writ," means nothing to you *as the author*. Because, most assuredly you can and often must go back, erase, rewrite, revise, change, until at last you are satisfied. To you, the author, the time interval of your story is really a spatial, rather than a true time distance. You plan your story, let us say, to cover two months in the life of your central character. Just so, but then, instead of two months of ordinary time, you, as the author, have a canvas two months long—just as it might be two yards long—on which you may paint and repaint as you please.

It may appear that I am overdoing it when I repeat as often as I have done the matter of viewpoint. But so stubbornly does the sense of clock time cling to us all, so deep is our conviction that we can do nothing at all with real (i.e., past) time, that all this repetition is necessary. Or at least I have found it so in working with students. For purposes of illustration, let us draw for ourselves another small picture here, to show the distinction between time as it is to actual people, including your central character, and as it is to you, the author:

$$\text{Past} . 1 . . \text{P}^1 . . \left\{ \begin{array}{l} \text{Object "A"} \\ \text{Event or} \end{array} \right\} . . \text{P}^2 . . \left\{ \begin{array}{l} \text{Object "B"} \\ \text{Event or} \end{array} \right\} . . \text{P}^3 . . 2 . \text{Future}$$

Your story, let us say, has begun at 1, to the left, and eventually will end at 2, over to the right. This distance from 1 to 2 is the space of time you plan to let your story cover. You have written the first few paragraphs, and just now your VP character, carrying with him that *human* way of seeing reality only in things behind him, is at P^1. Well, how is the event or object happening at A, in his future, going to look to him?

You, the author, know very well what it looks like to you. But you are standing outside the story, looking at it from a vastly different angle. How is your character, in the plane of the story, going to "see" that (to him) future event?

Obviously, it must present to him the exceedingly misty shape of something to come. It looks to him at P^1 just as something you expect to happen to you tomorrow or the next day looks to you now. And you must so write it at P^1 point in your story.

But what about the way the same object or event looks by the time your VP character has progressed to position P^2, past the event?

At P^2 your VP character can look two ways. He can look back across what is now (to him) *real* time, that is, time in his past, and, in the manner of objective science, see the object or event as a dead, unchangeable object. (And note, please, that this reverse side of the event may, and probably does, look very different from what he saw at position P^1—from what he anticipated, that is.)

Or the VP character can turn around and look forward again, to Event B, which must be described in the same dreamy, misty, shape-of-something-or-other-to-come manner we used for the appearance of Event A at position P^1. But not the way we talked about Event A at position P^2!

Next, what happens when the VP character moves on to position P^3 and has both Event A and Event B in his real, unchangeable past? The answer is that he now sees the back, or "real" (materially speaking, of course) sides of both events. But from this position Event B partially or completely obscures Event A; or, at the least, it changes the picture materially. This also you must bear in mind when writing it.

Even so, simply to say that Event A, for example, must be described differently from position P^1 than from position P^2 does not tell the writer just *what* that difference is and how to get at it. So that we may visualize the difference, let us examine another picture:

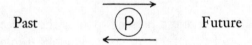

Past   P   Future

Here we have a magnified picture of that tiny traveling point, P, the present. We have enlarged it enough to discover that it is really a little wheel, rolling from past to future across our space line of time. Now examine the highly significant, simultaneous, yet opposed movements of the rolling wheel.

At the bottom of the wheel, against the hard material reality of the road, the direction of movement is actually toward the rear, toward the past, is it not?

Time and reality seem to spin out from the contact, flowing in an unbroken stream toward the remote past, just as they seem to do in real life. And if you were a dwarf, standing on the rim of the wheel and facing in the direction of movement (as you naturally would), at the bottom you would be looking to the rear, the past. And that is also where you would be closest to hard material reality, is it not?

In other words, you would be seeing objectively. It amounts to looking backwards with mud in your eye—just as you have been taught by a material education.

But what about the top of the wheel, where the movement is in the opposite direction, towards the front, the future?

Here you, as the tiny seeing eye on the rim, would not only be looking to the future but would also be lifted the entire diameter of the wheel above the dusty, obscuring materialism, the reverse "reality" of the bottom. Yes, but still, *how does one look to the future in so many words?*

One does it with one's emotional eye. Reread the sample objective and subjective paragraphs on our little friend, *M. mephitis,* given near the beginning of this chapter. In the objective paragraph our imaginary scientist looks backward at the drab, dead materials, the tangible things which he presumes were the polecat. But in the subjective paragraph our equally imaginary fictionist looks forward at the same animal. "Horrid suspicion," "I was tempted." "How this will come out—" These are your phrases for looking forward.

Our emotions, our hopes, fears, desires, joys, loves, even our hates—all these look primarily to the future. And these are the intangibles from which life is evolved, from which life begins.

Always, in natural order, the object comes after the subject, remember. You push on the top of a wheel, not the bottom, to start it rolling forward. You start with the subjective to get to the objective. It is the subjective that drives, that makes us *be* and *will* and *go* somewhere and *do* things. And this is true also for story.

Subjective, objective—any moving force, including a piece of fiction, necessarily must have them both. All moving forces move in a closed circuit, a cycle, a wheel moving simultaneously in opposed directions. Light, moving through curved space, for a tremendous example. The earth, revolving about the sun and rotating as it revolves. The current in the wires which supplies the power to the electric lights above you. I, in my life, you in yours; and so also our characters in the mimic, paper world we create for them and call story. You cannot have either a wheel or a story turning only in one direction, moving on but one side.

And this leads us to a fundamental principle of correct fiction writing:

There must be movement in two directions, a fact (looking and rolling backward) and a feeling (looking and moving forward) in virtually every sentence of your story.

This is the subjective method of handling space and time. You do not have to be so mechanically precise, of course, that every single sentence, however brief, fulfills the law. Sometimes the feeling may be in one sentence and the correlated fact in the next, or vice versa. Sometimes the feeling will be merely implied; sometimes, though must more rarely, it will be the fact that is implied. But you must always keep the wheel spinning on both sides, with the drive on the subjective side. You do it, I mean, something like this:

> Angrily he whirled. The dark figure behind him had not moved, had not made a sound. But now the sullen lids were wide open and the dull eyes had a chill, basilisk stare to them, like the eyes of a great snake. Something incredibly evil in that silent stare, something smirking, something filled with cold, nameless

horrors. A thin chill seeping through him, Don grinned back with his lips only, and swung toward the door.

Note that three of the five sentences begin with the emotional component, the "feeling." "Angrily he . . ." "Something incredibly evil . . ." "A thin chill seeping . . ." We are putting the impetus, the power, primarily on the top of the wheel as we should, powering the story forward. Yet, at the same time, we are not neglecting the backward moving bottom of our wheel, and in every sentence there is also a fact, an objective description either of an action or of a physical appearance.

Note further that each sentence begins differently—just as no two revolutions of a moving wheel begin exactly the same. By this constant change we convey the feeling of movement and avoid the monotony which inevitably accompanies a wheel that spins on a fixed pivot, getting nowhere. Each sentence also "hooks" into the preceding and succeeding sentences without a break.

Adverbs, adjectives, comparisons, metaphors are employed to present the emotions; and sometimes these emotions are only implied. "The dark figure behind him had not moved." ". . . the sullen lids were wide open . . ." ". . . the dull eyes . . ." These look like objective descriptions, but they are not. For, obviously, there is no reason at all for inserting them, save to picture the actually unpicturable emotional state inside our VP character, namely the feeling of crouching evil.

And, finally, the paragraph is "going somewhere." We know by the way it moves. The fine point of focused attention alternates, top–bottom, top–bottom, round and round, just as the dwarf, riding the rim, would "see" a moving wheel. We, the readers, feel that the story is moving, and yet—reverting to ordinary concepts of time and space—we notice how submerged is the fact that we have moved the VP character across a time interval of at least a minute or two and a space of, say, the length of the room.

As the authors, or creators, we are superior to earthly time and space. To us it is as nothing, and a thousand years are but a watch in the night. For we can easily let our VP character live a whole eternity in the second he stares back into those malevolent eyes. Or we can have the evil eyes catch him up in their dark spell, hurl him out into infinite, icy space as his senses fade. We, the creators, are limited only by our own ability to imagine and convey our dream to that absorbed ghost, the reader.

The Wandering Jew, condemned to wander through eternity, *Buck Rogers in the Twenty-fifth Century*, *The Magic Carpet*, *The Seven League Boots*, *Aladdin's Lamp* —these and all the other delightful people and properties of fiction old and new—are they not made superior to earthly time and space, made so by their authors? And do we not *believe* as we read? It is a great magic that you have there in your mind!

As a working rule, cut every objective description or account of physical action which does not carry a strong counterpoint of emotion of the kind you need to build up your problem, but seldom eliminate or pass over the emotion. By adhering to this rule, you will find ordinarily yourself handling space and time problems quite satisfactorily, and along with them the problem of transitions.

"For the letter killeth, but the spirit giveth life," is a precept that was written especially and particularly for writers. The words you must use, being in themselves dead objects, are not your story at all. Be miserly with them, use not one more than you must; and when you are tempted, remember the automobile-battery comparison. If the battery in your automobile goes dead, you remove it and replace it with another, rather than leave it, perhaps with many of its predecessors, simply to occupy space. No one attached greater importance to the *right* word in fiction than Joseph Conrad, and no one, perhaps struggled more than he to achieve it, with a success that may readily be seen in his works.

In the experience of a considerable number of fiction writers whom I have questioned over a period of years, I have found that by far the most favorable time to "see" a story is either just before or just after sleep, with a decided preference for the former.

That is understandable, of course. Fiction stories are merely manufactured dreams, just another of the myriad of synthetic products of our time, *psychosynthetics*, if you please. And the dreams one remembers, natural or synthetic, generally do come in the half-asleep, half-awake state. However miraculous one's first experience in thus "seeing" a story may seem—"seeing" it perhaps with no more effort than one uses to look at a face, after bitter, fruitless days trying to "work it out"—all of this is perfectly normal and natural.

But exceedingly intriguing is the fact that most of such stories are "seen" in the peaceful pause just before one drops into the sleep so much like the greater sleep of death. For there we are moving away from the material world toward something else; there, like Moses, we are permitted to look, at least, onward into a better land and to hear perhaps the bright accounts. There we may ask and expect to receive. For in our dreams, at least, we are fabulous and free.

III

On Character

And no man understands any greatness or goodness
but his own, or the indication of his own.

WALT WHITMAN

IN using the subjective method advanced in this book,
you will find it impossible to separate successfully your
character from his plot problems and keep either real.
The two simply go together, or the one inevitably suggests the other. But, since the lay reader, like the much
maligned imaginary scientist dissecting *M. mephitis*, never quite realizes this essential dualism and demands the
tangible while actually looking for the intangible, you
will need to know more about this problem of apparently
writing one thing but meaning another.

We are primarily concerned in a fiction story (as distinguished from a fact story) with proving by illustration,
by a parable, that a given conflict of emotions can be
solved by proper application of the appropriate moral
principle. Only secondarily are we interested in creating
a vehicle, a character, to carry the load. But the reader
almost always thinks he is much more interested in the
character than in the problem!

The truth is, of course, that the reader is interested in
his own inner self and that self's problems. Unconsciously,
and more or less completely (depending upon how well
we have handled our VP work), he identifies that inner
self with the inner self of the VP character. He senses in
the VP character a kindred soul, and so he willingly be-

comes a part of the VP trinity, consisting of that living "Me" in which author, character and reader are indistinguishably merged. Yes, but what really persuades him to join that union and stick with it to the very end?

It is not the scant possibility that we have created our VP character to fit the reader's physical characteristics, certainly, for there is not one chance in a thousand that we have. Perhaps one individual reader of our story will be a boy of fifteen; and the next a woman of seventy! How do we cut our physical cloth to fit both of these extremes? Or even achieve a usable compromise? We can't, and neither can we create a static "kindred soul" to turn the trick. What does a "kindred soul" look like and how do we know that it resembles the soul of our reader, fifteen or seventy, or that he or she will like it even though it is his or her "spit'n image"?

Despite all the folk who mistakenly insist that good fiction writing is objective reporting or psychoanalysis or something else, you know better by now. You know that the way to capture the reader and incorporate him into the VP "Me" is not by attempting the impossible, by trying to describe him statically and objectively. Instead, you do it by adopting him *subjectively*.

I mean, you know that misery loves company. You know that men band together in adversity—cling even closer than brothers—and later fight over the loot of victory. You know that the most joyous intellectual impulse that comes to the average man occurs when he sees a brother struggling with a problem and can exclaim eagerly, "Oh, I know, I know! Let *me* try!"

Very well, let him try! Make him a comrade in adversity with yourself and your VP character. How? By picking a problem with which he feels he is at least familiar, something he has struggled with, something within his moral understanding.

That is the problem we are talking about, observe. The $1 + 1$ or $1 - 1$ equation; the *honor + love = ?;* or *duty + fear;* or *pride — miserliness;* or whatever. But what about the character—that vehicle—to carry the problem? How do you create him?

You do it in essentially the same way that you create story. Primarily, character is created by conflict, and the stronger the conflict the stronger the character. Further, the stronger the character the more eagerly your readers will pay to see him, the more readily they will identify themselves with him.

Observe how many millions who never saw South Bend, Indiana, are nevertheless fanatic partisans, brothers-in-arms, of the Notre Dame football team. Or of Minnesota, or Army, Navy, or one of the other pigskin greats. Pit Notre Dame against Army or Minnesota or Texas, and scores of thousands will pay to watch, millions will listen—why?

Because you have achieved the epitome of interest, mighty driving force against almost indomitable resistance. You have created a characterful struggle.

Why is a bottle of lemon soda on the shelf given scarcely a glance, while a bottle of nitroglycerin—straw-colored stuff which appears much the same—is accorded tremendous respect and attention? It is because we know there is no real power, no conflict in the lemon soda. But nitro—that is different!

Locked in terrific struggle within that palish fluid, we know, are two tremendous antagonists, an almost inconceivably explosive force held in check by a molecular force so slightly superior that a mere careless touch on our part, even a hard look perhaps, may be enough to break the deadlock and unleash a roaring tide of destruction. Well, that is the way to create vital, dynamic, compelling characters in your story.

Make compounds that could go off. Sodawater, perhaps, with a faint pop for your weaklings, your very minor characters, but a stick of dynamite for your central character. You do not necessarily have to explode him all over the reader to prove his potency, of course. But make your main character a stick of giant, nevertheless, and never let the reader forget it.

Further, in compounding your character, bear in mind the particular story problem for which you are making him. You compound him, for example, of pride and love if the story problem is to be pride and love. The Sire de Malétroit was quite a stick of dynamite—fiercely proud, fiercely fond of his niece, and as such was an exceedingly dangerous man when young Denis crossed him. Of what avail would it have been to Stevenson to make his hero proud and miserly, as did Maupassant in his tale, *A Piece of String?* A miserly character would not have exploded all over young Denis for a love mix-up apparently besmirching the family honor. Nor would a proud yet loving Maître Hauchecorne have cared very much had his neighbors (whom he would have loved had his character been pride-love) chaffed him about picking up the bit of string.

You make your central character fit the story problem and the story problem fit the central character. In other words, they are inseparable, unified; the character inevitably suggests the story problem, the story problem suggests the character.

You must do this in your imagination before you start putting character and story on paper. Remember, we are going to prove what the character is in the story itself. Do not take dull forever in the story to compound the character before the testing and the fireworks start. Just bring him in boldly labeled "Dynamite," with the explosive ingredients, "Equal parts of pride and love," for example, printed on the wrapper. In that way you get for him instant respect and attention.

To say this in another way, one of the most common of all beginning writers' faults is to have the characters born on page 1, full grown physically perhaps, but psychically without any past or problems, and accordingly without any character. Then it is necessary to wade through page after page of dull copy, while the author grinds and mixes the ingredients which should have been completely mixed, molded, and fused as the written story began. *Don't make this mistake in your stories, ever!*

Mix your powder in the laboratory of your own imagination before you move on to the location of your blasting job. A story that takes ten pages to compound the characters before the supreme testing starts simply will not sell. Don't be guilty of such careless amateurism.

Give each one of your characters a past. Imagine this past vividly, make it real in your own mind before you start to write the character into your story. And give the character a dominating, emotional-problem make-up, a compound that will fit in with the particular use to which you intend to put the character.

Let us illustrate this by using old Father Abraham again, for a splendid example, in our prime 1 + 1 story:

As the chapter (the "short story") opens, we know very definitely that Abraham is an intensely religious man, in close communion with his God. How do we know? Does the author take ten pages to describe Abraham's nature? He definitely does not; he says, instead, *in the very first sentence*, that, tempting Abraham, God said to him, "Abraham!" and Abraham answered instantly, "Here I am."

Very well, a man to whom God speaks and who answers at once patently must be in close communion with his God. No static, objective description is needed. The dynamic action tells the tale. And in the very next sentence, the Lord again speaking, "Take now thy son, thine only son Isaac, whom thou lovest . . . and offer him . . . for a burnt offering."

There is the other essential ingredient of Abraham's character, one which, again, is not flatly and drearily described, but, instead, is included in a swift, dynamic command. But let us consider what this means.

The objective description is not there. But, even had we read nothing else about Abraham, we can still picture him, can't we? Our imagination supplies the details. Here is a man who loves his God and his family, as well. Love of the spirit, love of the flesh, and is there a one of us who does not know what this means! Inner conflict! The lusty, driving forces of the flesh forever hammering against the stern resistance of religion! Against the surging urge, an equally imperious, "Thou shalt not!" We know without being told a word more. Abraham's character, in so far as it interests us in this story, is compounded of love of God *versus* love of the flesh. And this story will deal not with the compounding of this character, but instead with the putting of it to the supreme test.

Subtly, we are even told what the probable outcome will be, are we not? A man in as close communion with his God as Abraham is probably will obey his God. But the test, now—to sacrifice the supreme exemplification of his earthly life, the flesh of his flesh, bone of his bone, blood of his blood, his only beloved son, if he is to obey the Lord. What does Abraham do?

He acts in character. He does not stop to analyze or rationalize, for if he did so he would end by doing nothing at all. Instead, he does what we instinctively expect an intensely religious man to do. In good faith, he puts Isaac on the altar and starts to sacrifice him.

And yet, had he not loved Isaac devotedly, had there been no conflict of emotions within him before the story starts, had he not been a bundle of contradictions, what value, what interest, in the test?

Think of a sword maker testing a blade he has just made. Bright, keen, shining, tempered, but what does he do with it? He bends it in a semicircle to see if it will break, slashes it savagely against a heavy block to see if the edge will dull. Yet he wants it not to bend when the swordsman thrusts, he wants it not to dull when the swordsman cuts. Why does he try to bend, break, or dull it?

Because he knows the blade must successfully combine contradictory characteristics. Stiffness and yet flexibility. The razor sharpness of glass, and yet not glass's brittleness. An edge that will both cut and, when it cannot cut, still refuse to be blunted. Doesn't this tell us something we have known all our lives and yet, perhaps, have failed to realize until this moment?

Do not hesitate for an instant to give your hero or heroine lusts of the flesh, dark passions, impulses to evil, or whatever you may call them. For these dark powers, fused with their opposites—the will to good, the moral impulses, the powers of the spirit—will do to your character precisely what the opposite powers of fire and water do to the sword blade. The sword maker first heats his blade red hot, then quenches it in water to temper it, does he not?

Do not forget, your true story is within, not without, your central character. The real reason for bringing the sword to the testing block is not to see the sparks fly, not to enjoy the exciting spectacle of a brawny man flailing a heavy chunk of wood with a fine, expensive sword, although these, indeed, are what we see. Nevertheless, the idea, the real reason for the spectacle, is to test the metal inside the blade, *the fused contradictions* which we cannot see but know to exist.

And the whole success or failure of the performance, whether we are to judge it a triumph or a tragedy, hinges on the performance of those unseen contradictions, on whether the blade passes or fails the test.

The reason for greater rejoicing in heaven over the rescue of one lusty, repentant sinner than over ninety-nine shining saints is simply that the repentant sinner is worth more than the saints. He is steel to their pot metal. He has faced and fought the temptations they never knew; he has lost and picked himself up from the flat of his back and fought again, and won! He is, in short, a man, and you like that kind of character instinctively.

Then write about that kind of character and dismiss the saintly ones! Make your characters terrifically good and horribly bad at the same time, allowing the good to win out after struggles, temptations, and agonies.

Let us look at some actual people, now, in order to fix the meaning of this need for contradiction—for conflict within—to create compelling character. How about Theodore Roosevelt?

A puny, sickly, asthmatic child, with weak eyes, surely young T. R. must have seemed poor material for a great character. But, within that frail body was a driving spirit, a big force, a tremendous zest for life. And see what happened!

He made of himself a great man. It is not recorded that he got drunk, or habitually overate, or gave way to wild fits of rage, or in any other way yielded utterly to those ebullient animal spirits within him. But nobody ever doubted that he could have done all those things, and efficiently, too. Everybody knew that T. R. got a terrific kick out of life, that when he was on hand everything would be "bully!" or, by all that's holy, he would see that it was made so! Everyone respected him, whether he approved of him or not. All of this because everyone sensed that, within the man, there was terrific power held in masterly restraint.

His strong teeth and eyeglasses became a sort of trademark for American vitality and action. Yet no one seems to have noted the contradiction in these two aspects of the man—strong animal teeth and eye glasses (crutches for weak eyes). However, taken together, they were no sign of weakness or dissension. They were, instead, the ideograph, the character symbol, of a dynamic, well-rounded character, a great American.

And assuredly there is more than the mere smell of dynamite in his famous axiom for American conduct: "Speak softly and carry a big stick." There is obvious analogy here with the most dramatic of all American stock characters, the Southern Colonel (sometimes transplanted to the West), who is deadly only when he drops his voice.

Consider also Abraham Lincoln. He was physically ugly, or so his enemies said. He was poor; he was without formal education, without family background, without place or pomp or circumstance or influence to aid him; and he was married to a woman whom many considered an extravagant shrew. So bitter were her diatribes against him in the presence of embarrassed outsiders, that poor Lincoln, away from home attending circuit courts, would often stay away during the recesses and interims, enduring the atrocious, early Illinois country-town hotels, rather than go home to face Mrs. Lincoln. And at forty, by his own admission, he considered himself a failure.

Do you think he was never embarrassed, humiliated, bitter, or resentful? Do you suspect for an instant that the stinging barbs of his enemies—and they called him every vile name in and out of the book—didn't hurt?

How would you have felt, a shy, awkward, ugly backwoods lawyer, compelled to face the polished contempt, the well-tutored sophistication, all the deadly batteries of fame and birth and breeding of such an antagonist as Stephen A. Douglas? Or the infinitely less gentlemanly epithets of a Vallandigham, or the snarling contempt of a Stanton?

Yet he did not retaliate, no matter how powerful his enraged, humiliated impulse to repay in kind or worse; and there is no denying that he had the impulses. He was human, even as you and I. Even his sorrows—and he had them, both public and private, in overwhelming measure —he kept to himself, shunting them off by praying in the privacy of his study or by offering a joke, some gentle, inoffensive humor, to his incessant callers, even his bitterest enemies.

As we count material blessings in this world, he had nothing, and life gave him nothing, save a bitter cup filled to the brim. And yet, out of that nothing he made a tremendous something, an American character, a dream and a memory to stir men's souls until the name of the United States is not even a dim scrawl on the last known page from the past.

"He that loseth his life shall find it," says the Good Book. "He that humbleth himself shall be exalted." The ugly shall be handsome, just as Lincoln is considered now. The weak shall become figures of strength, like T. R. For similar transformations, we need not go beyond our own generation and time, which now are producing characters as strong and as striking as those of any other era.

Do you begin to see how character formula is but story formula in another aspect, and vice versa—that they roll into one, into the all-inclusive, subjective "Me"? And here we are confronted by the time and space problem again, likewise in a new aspect.

What about right and left, forwards and backwards, good and evil, or any other forces that you may name, positive and negative? How shall you, as author, deal with these?

You must learn, in creating, or "plotting," your story world, at least, to stand beyond good and evil, regarding them as impartially as a scientist looks at nitric acid and glycerin when he prepares to compound nitroglycerin, or as fairly as an honest referee considers the two contending football teams in a game for which he is responsible. This, to be sure, is not easy.

It is worse than that. It is probably impossible for the average individual, trained as he is to follow precept and precedent and give instant lip service to the cause of righteousness, to realize that even sin may have its uses and place. This last, however, is a valid point of view in writing and has nothing to do with the principles of morals which most professional writers adhere to in private life. I wish merely to point out that, in the worlds of sports and stories, at least, it takes two to make a fight. Not only that, but we must write about a fight, or better still, several fights, and these fights must be good ones.

The world's champion against the leading challenger, or the nation's top football team against the one in second position—these are the fights that fill the stadiums, bowls, and halls, and likewise the pages of the best paying fiction magazines. There is little logic but much feeling in our choice of sides in real life, but that is beside the point. Which of two antagonists is the "enemy" depends almost altogether upon which side we choose to sit. But in writing, something more is needed.

As the creator and judge of your fiction world, you must try to see both sides—you must be fair, even to the devil; you must never be blindly partisan, even in behalf of the most manifest virtue and goodness. To do otherwise is to detract, perhaps fatally, from the dramatic intensity of the struggle you are attempting to depict.

It must be remembered that the shining spires of heaven are erected upon the dark but enduring foundations of hell. The height of the angels is measured from the depth of the demons below. And neither of these places or beings is real without the other. Permit your hero or heroine to champion good, if you wish (it is not necessary in many modern markets but it is very much preferred by all of the more opulent ones), but never permit him or her to fight against nothing.

Forward and back, positive and negative, good and evil—however you wish to see the eternal wheel, the conflict of life—always bear in mind that *both sides are forces*. The negative is also a force, in the opposite direction. Make it so, and give it its full innings. For the more successfully you do so, the better your story will be.

A strongly moral hero, unassailed by any of the strong seductions of sin, is the poorest of all characters with which to essay a story, simply because he is not a character at all. You cannot really have a force, save in relation to an opposing force, a resistance. You cannot really have a wheel that turns forward only, on the upper, "spiritual" side and ignores all necessity for simultaneous backward motion on the bottom, against the material road. No one will believe you if you claim impossible qualities for your hero, even though you may have devised means to "test" the paragon.

But, proceeding from impossibilities to improbabilities, sometimes you can palm off a story using the next worst kind of hero. He is that distressing flat wheel, the one-sided character, a force indeed, but with his opposing force furnished almost altogether by external agencies.

This flat wheel is the dummy one finds puppeting for the hero in the very cheapest of the cheap pulp magazines.

He is Mister Goodman and is terribly mistreated by Brother Badfellow, another flat wheel, of course, but on the other side. When these two wheels get together, the necessary opposing forces do clash, it is true, and you do have a species of story. But it is primitive, coarse-weave stuff that ordinarily will satisfy only the simplest of reader minds.

But let us go a step higher and make our hero character very definitely real and human, that is, *both* good and bad, as he enters the story. He is still extraordinarily good, let us presume, and his genuine temptations accordingly are few and far between. We still must supply most of the villainous opposition externally. We must, that is, have a villain who is three-fourths or more bad and only incidentally good, and to that extent human. We still shall require very loud and violent physical action to resolve the story. But we do not have to make it quite as violent as we must when Mr. All-Good meets and destroys Brother Plumbad. And definitely we have a better, more real, and more appealing story. We are moving up out of the very cheapest markets, I mean, and beginning to learn our business. Suppose we now move still another step upward and make our hero character a man almost exactly balanced between the storming forces of good and evil. Now what?

Now we know that he must be a casuist, for one thing; a man who is not only trying to do the right thing, but who also wonders what is right, and occasionally tries to reason himself into believing that perhaps part of what appears to be bad really is good, or vice versa. He is still more like an ordinary human being; I mean, more *real*. And we have in him a character whom we do not have to attack with roaring sixguns, whooping road agents, hell-for-leather outlaws, and similar pulp accessories to make him explode or pass the test. Here is a character whose intensely dramatic inner conflict we can test and resolve with only a minimum of outside aid and motion.

Just a little something—a matter of dropping the bottle of nitroglycerin two inches to see whether it goes off—turns the trick. And the result is "slick" character and "slick" story, as distinguished from "pulp" character and "pulp" story. It is the kind of tale the top-paying "slick" magazines want but seldom get. It is also very difficult to write, not because of any lack of writers who can write good characters, but because so few can make a character extraordinarily good and bad at one and the same time.

Let us go the whole distance and imagine a character perfectly balanced between good and evil, a hero in whom the vitalizing contradictions are so perfectly matched, so deadlocked, that he actually doesn't know which is which, or what side he is on. To be sure, this would be a remarkably good story if one could write it. Practically no one can, though many try. It is the ideal of the "quality-story" market, so called, and it accounts for the astonishingly large number of 1 — 1 formulas you find in quality periodicals. They are tales in which the poor hero ends up by hanging himself by his own emotional tie, or even worse, simply fighting himself into nothing, like the famous Kilkenny cats. Don't do this kind of story unless you just simply must.

The good reason for avoiding it (aside from the fact it doesn't pay very well, even when you sell) is that such a character as this walks the ragged edge of the abyss and, with one false step, falls in. An effete, effeminate group, top-heavy with undigested, objective culture, may, and indeed probably does, form a large percentage of your reader audience for such tales, whereas only a scant minority of fine minds will be able to appreciate your perfect balancing feat. One too-strenuous effort to cater to this parasite group, one misstep, and down you go into fictional perversion, all of your fictional purpose and pattern reversed, the devil quoting Scripture for his own purposes.

Against the sewage flood of obscenity masquerading as fiction, stories, so called, appealing brazenly to sexual perverts, sadists, masochists, and homosexuals, may be matched in full stench and measure the equally perverted "quality" stories which have cursed our times. And these so-called "quality" tales, it should be remembered, *came first*, pointing the trend.

I do not wish to be misunderstood, however. I am not referring to the genuine quality story, whether it be plus or minus. But if there is any purpose or meaning to fiction, it must be that of guiding us, as Moses did, to a brighter, better world, a place ahead in which those who live will be more complete. Any reversal of this dominant purpose, any perverted fad for building parables to preach futility and doom, will defeat itself.

Here beside me as I write are several collections of so-called "best" stories, all following the same dreary pattern. Inevitably the central character displays a pathetic unfamiliarity with his environment. If he is a farmer, he doesn't know about strayed stock laws or how to stretch fence wire; if he is an oil man, he doesn't know that a walking beam is *not* a headache post and that you *can't* blithely walk into a burning gusher; if the heroine lives on the lower Rio Grande, she has small children *wading* across the river. The psychiatrists, I think, call this sort of thing *loss of contact with environment*.

When this symptom is joined with the unvarying (though often perverted) 1 — 1 story formula through which these miserable characters wade, moving from something to nothing, disintegration of personality emerges almost inevitably. And loss of contact with environment and disintegration of personality are the two distinguishing characteristics of schizophrenia, the mental ailment currently filling our asylums.

Somehow, I doubt that a reasonably rational people will long continue to purchase and pay for such patterns for going mad. And the taste for such stories is, I hope, a craze already at dead end. We might do well, therefore, to stick to more stable character creations in this, our little dissertation on how to live with, as well as on, what we write.

After all, dynamite, and not the far more unstable nitroglycerin, is the common article of commerce. Even when it is given medicinally as a heart stimulant, nitro-glycerin is administered very cautiously, in minute doses. There is a tip for us here, in handling our own equally explosive heart stimulants. But how do we go about making our reader appreciate the less explosive dynamite in our character—how do we make him realize what a power character we are offering him?

We do it simply, by saying that the character is dyna-mite—"Please Handle With Extreme Care"—as he enters the story. And observe the direction in which that warning looks.

Instead of considering our dynamite character as an object—I mean, looking backward and giving a dull account of just how the explosive was made—we look the other way. "Watch out!" we warn sharply. "Here's a stick of giant powder, a terrific affair. What do you think will happen when I drop it, or maybe even shoot into it, *as I'm going to do right now!*"

That gets the reader.

Then we go ahead with the tense business of putting the stick of dynamite, the character, through the test, still without any long dissertation on chemical constituents and manufacturing processes.

We do our best to paralyze the reader—freeze him to

the book. All quivering helplessness, he waits to see what is going to happen next. *What is going to happen next*, please note, not *what has happened!* We weave our spell and get the reader in our power before we start telling him about the ingredients and manufacturing processes that have made this stick of dynamite we are already putting to the test.

And even then we tell these dead details subjectively, in the guise of terrifically important facts reinforcing the deadly tension of the present. We do it with something of the technique of a carnival sideshow barker making his spiel. Like this:

"Looka, looka, looka, ladies and gentlemen, look at that stick of dynamite! Made of the purest glycerin money can buy, the most powerful nitric acid the laboratories of science can offer! Practically pure nitro, ladies and gentlemen, pure death and destruction, think of it! Why, even the sawdust exploded in the mill and killed four men! And now I'm going to shoot into this death-dealing demon of destruction, shoot right into it with a .45 to see what happens. Hold on to your hearts, folks, hold on, here goes . . . !"

You will have noted how little the above resembles the objectively scientific, "Dynamite is a commercial explosive obtained by absorbing nitroglycerin in some porous material. Nitroglycerin, $C_3H_5(NO_3)_3$, a nitrate of glycerol, is obtained by treating glycerol with a mixture of nitric and sulphuric acids." And yet, in abbreviated form, this is what the subjective paragraph also tells you, save that it looks forward, rather than backward. The information is there, either way. But the all-important difference is the direction from which you look at it.

Let us now try this briefly in a real story, that of Abraham and Isaac. We will assume that we have already told our readers that Abraham, a devoutly religious man, has received the Lord's command to sacrifice Isaac, and now has decided to go to the mount, at least that far before finally making up his mind. The scene:

> There was black agony in Abraham's breast as he hesitated. He looked down into the boy's small, brown, trusting face. "Come on, son," he said, and choked at the youngster's instant obedience.
>
> "But, father—" Bewilderment clouded the brown eyes even as a small, chubby hand came thrusting confidingly into Abraham's own. "The . . . the sacrifice? Aren't you—won't we have to take—something? If the Lord says . . ."
>
> There it was, and Abraham closed his eyes. The tearing pain! When a man has obeyed all his life, when he has fought the good fight, followed the Way, why then the deep, worn grooves of discipline are not to be denied. But to take a man's son, his only son! That . . . .
>
> "We're going to find something, are we, dad?" The small fingers lay in warm peace in the large ones and there was perfect faith on the upturned face. Faith and trust and a tiny, eager smile. A man child, a son, an *only* son, solace of old age. Wanted so long. The black horror caught again.
>
> "Son!" All sudden, savage rebellion, Abraham caught the small hand in both his, starting to scream, to rave out his refusal and fury. But out there in the black was the Flame. Perfect, shining, ineffable Light, beyond all dark, beyond good and evil, hope or fear, beyond it all. "Yes, son, yes." The small fingers curled confidingly and Abraham took an uncertain, almost stumbling step. "We'll find—we'll—find something . . . ."

This is no attempt to improve the Bible. It is a simplification—an over-simplification—of a pattern. The emotional overtones, particularly, are exaggerated, so that you may see them. But it should be noted that the essential, objective facts, namely, that Abraham has been a devout man all of his life, that he has hitherto obeyed the Lord without question, that this is his only son and comfort in his old age—all of these are stated. They are present but disguised as subjective details, reinforcements pointing up and strengthening the stormy conflict in the present. And there is only a hint of flashback.

The third sentence in the third paragraph, "When a man has obeyed all his life," etc., and the fourth in the fourth, "A man child," etc., are flashback sentences, since they plainly imply that Abraham is remembering details from the past. Quite often you will find it necessary to amplify this flashback reinforcing of present emotional conflict by having your character remember whole episodes, or connected chains of facts, from his past. But when you do introduce such flashbacks, always suspect them of being excess baggage, always prune ruthlessly on first versions and always bear in mind that they have no place whatever in your story, save to heighten the emotional conflict in the present.

Always deal with flashbacks subjectively, that is. Put them in at the exact place and time that your VP character would naturally remember them. Never forget that you are not primarily recording the facts, but, instead, the VP character in the act of remembering. Do not fall into dead, historical, objective rendering of the facts.

Since the VP character typically is the central character as well, I have here tacitly assumed as much in stating these essentials of character building technique. Obviously, in stories in which the central character is not the VP character, some small modifications are necessary. But, as a general thing, all I have said continues to hold good.

Whether you elect to place the VP trinity inside your main character or elsewhere, you still must introduce that main character with a "Dynamite" label. You must start to put him to the supreme and appropriate test *before* you give detailed reminiscences of how he happened to have such a character conflict in the first place.

How about the other characters in your story?

Well, each of them, in appropriately lesser measure, must meet the same requirements. Make it a working rule never to bring anybody into a story to play an active part until you have first "created" him by vividly sensing, at least, both sides of his character conflict, both forces at war within him, both forward moving top and backward moving bottom of his wheel of life.

Only the spear bearers, cowboys, posses, mobs and the like need not be vitalized by contradiction; but even they will be improved by brief exposure to the process. Consider how our language abounds in clichés that bring things to life by teamings of opposites:

"Cowardly mob." "Good little devil." "Chivalrous foe." "Little giant." "Beloved enemy." And so on. Two words in combination have the power to bestow life; one alone may not.

How many characters are needed in a story?

That is difficult to answer specifically. But it is certain that you must not use one more than you actually need to fulfill your purpose, the supreme testing of your central character, to the satisfaction of your reader. Theoretically, it should be possible to write an excellent story using only one character, the hero. But it is so hard to do that you almost never see such a tale.

Nowadays you will need ordinarily at least two main characters, a hero and a villain. But it is even better practice, even in the action pulps, to have three, a hero, heroine, and villain, for in the end you can reward one of your virtuous characters by presenting him with the other, thus effecting a considerable saving of your space, time, and story energy.

You may, of course, have even more active characters, assistant heroes, heroines, and villains, up to the limit of the scant space allowed you, or the numbers that you hope your readers can remember. But, again, it is much better to limit the number of main characters and offer quality rather than mere quantity.

Personify your forces of evil, incidentally; always have a personal villain, even though he does reform in the end. And you will have much better luck in selling your story. It is possible to write a correct story in which the hero contends only with the impersonal forces of darkness, with malignant fate, or blind destiny. The ancient Greeks used this device. Indeed, the devil was not completely personified until the Middle Ages, but he proved himself so useful that he has been much in evidence ever since. Use him! If you are going to incarnate good in your hero, as you must, then go the whole distance and incarnate evil in a villain, too.

Do not consider any worthy fiction market beneath you; no matter what magazine or editor likes your tales, do your sincerest best to give that buyer quality. Even the cheapest pulps wistfully appreciate a quality performance. That your central character for such a market needs must be a simple one, in no way keeps you from making him high quality in his class. Learn to be a craftsman in writing, remembering that a craftsman is one who takes pride not in the lofty place of his product, but instead in the superlative fitting of it to its intended place and purpose.

It is infinitely better to build a first-rate cottage than a second-rate palace. Even Michelangelo was not above painting ceilings, nor Ruskin too superior to write stories for little children. While as for the author of *Alice In*

Wonderland, a story written for one little girl—who, pray, remembers that he was also a very learned mathematician?

Perhaps you can write for the great and learned, perhaps not. But, if not, no matter. It is just as honorable and worthy to write for the little people's magazines, or the simplest pulps, as it is to produce "quality" magazine tales, and indeed it is probably more valuable. You will have a far more appreciative audience in the simpler markets, and a more faithful one.

Long ago the shrewd Jesuits realized that to produce the most profound effects in this world, to be sure of the permanence of what you would teach, you must catch your audience very young in spirit, if not also in years. We are interested in making our tales as nearly immortal as possible, are we not? Very well, who gets into the eternal kingdom of heaven?

The following simple working rules of characterization technique may be pasted over your typewriter:

(1) *Always* do a sincere job with your central character. Go all out, rage with him, despair, plumb the depths of his catastrophes and the heights of his ecstasies. To write this character with your tongue smugly in your cheek is always fatal.

(2) Always have a personal villain.

(3) Always make your character and your story fit, like hand and glove. Make the test, which constitutes the story, an appropriate one! You wouldn't test a sword by trying to put it through a cream separator, would you?

(4) Fit the other characters to your central character, as a rule, and not the other way around. I mean, having once got your story problem and the carrying central character in mind, do not change either of these just be-

cause some fascinating new character happens to pop into your mind. Change the new character to fit the problem and central character.

(5) Never use negative (in the sense of "do nothing") central characters. *Always* make this central character the one who *moves, decides, does.* And when anything acts on him, as it must, do not emphasize this action, but rather your character's reaction. Not, "He was stunned," for example. Write instead, "Stunned, he fought instinctively to break that paralysis, succeeded at last with a furious effort of will, and whirled to the attack."

(6) Tag all of your principal characters with at least two contradicting physical details suggesting the dominant inner conflict. Strong teeth and eyeglasses, for example. "A handsome face, except that the eyes were just a shade too close together"—a typical stock villain. "A plain, almost a petulant little face, except when she smiled." Ah, a heroine!

(7) And finally: Test each and every active character you use before you are finally satisfied with him.

The test of correct characterization is a "yes" answer to, "Could I put the viewpoint in this character's brain, tell *his* story complete, instead of sketchily as here, and *still have a good, correct story?*" If the answer is "no," *change the character.*

~IV~

The Parts and the Process

The Ball no Question makes of Ayes and Noes
But Right or Left as strikes the Player goes
   And He that toss'd Thee down into the Field
He knows about it all—HE knows—HE knows!

RUBAIYAT OF OMAR KHAYYAM

OBJECTIVELY, there are four parts to the correct short story: (1) situation, (2) complication, (3) crisis, (4) climax. There is one unvarying but reversible process, transcendent forward and back, plus and minus, sacrifice and redemption. But, in the contradictory nature of character, all of this must be contained and accomplished under apparent intent of telling and doing something else altogether.

You say one thing, actually meaning another. You do something whose real purpose may be the exact opposite of its seeming one. You guide yourself in this oftimes perplexing business of operating with contraries by adhering steadfastly to your fundamentals.

Never do you forget that in fiction you do not deal *primarily* with individual people as people, actions as actions, or even things as things. You may indeed speak of all these, appearing to be telling of casual cowboys, evanescent love affairs, or something else. But, actually, you are dealing *in a parable* with the eternal and ineffable verities, with the eternal, dubious battle on the plains of heaven, the timeless conflict of good and evil, the incessant clash of forces as ageless, spaceless, and formless as eternity itself.

"The Way which can be expressed in words is not the eternal Way; the Name which can be uttered is not the eternal Name." Thus the philosophers. And yet, if some small sense of this eternal Way and Name does not enter into our tale, however light and transient we may intend it, then we fail of our purpose.

We might look first at the part hardest to see, the dynamic process. We have already considered the static aspect of this technique in Chapter I, that is, the equations to which the problems can be reduced. Just so does the engineer reduce the flight of a bullet to a ballistics table, or the potentialities of an engine to so many mathematical formulas. But how different a bullet or an engine is in action!

What does story process look like dynamically?

In infinite variation, it looks like either the story of Abraham and Isaac or the story of Eve and the apple.

Always, in one variation or another, the central character is impaled on the horns of a seeming dilemma, caught between the grinding surfaces of two apparently irreconcilable emotions, desires, urges, or wants.

Always, after more or less prolonged and agonizing struggle, he comes to the final fork in the road, the spot where he must make the irrevocable choice: the spot of Abraham with the knife raised before the altar; or of Eve with the apple at her lips.

Always at this spot he *decides* and *does*. In the plus pattern story he makes the "right" (meaning morally right) choice and immediately acts to incarnate it. In the minus pattern he makes a "wrong" (or at least opposite of "right") decision and puts it into being by appropriate action.

And note here (and please pardon the repetition), be the decision and action either right or wrong, right or left, positive or negative, *they are always decision and action.*

78

That is, for example, the hero may decide to tell or not to tell some secret of vital importance to himself and others in the story. But, either way, he must *decide* and *do*. He must not be prevented from exercising his choice. If he decides to tell, *he does tell*; if he decides not to tell, *he has the opportunity* but *keeps his secret. Never* is he the helpless, impotent pawn of fate.

Ordinarily there comes next after this decision and action a more or less clearly defined *black moment*, that darkest period just before dawn, when it seems all is lost, the sacrifice is in vain, and so on.

And, finally, comes the answer or reward—*arrived at simply because the character took the "right" course at the instant of decision.* In the minus pattern plot, of course, the simple reverse of the plus type, the character decides on the sinister course, the wrong, the left-hand way, and so arrives at his punishment, his zero answer, the void beyond the black.

And this is all there is to story process.

Much easier to see are the gross parts of your story, for here at least you can count the pages and be reasonably sure. Just as in nature, a story, by divisions, is a dynamic, three-part affair, fused into a static, four-part arrangement.

By way of illustration, consider a year. You know that, dynamically speaking, a year consists of three parts. A season of life and growth, spring and summer, is followed by a season of decline, autumn, and that in turn by a third season of death, dead winter. But the static calendar divides this tripartite affair into four seasons, spring, summer, fall, and winter.

Just so with story. Dynamically, you have a beginning, middle, and end. But statically you have four parts, very readily identifiable, too, since in the normal story each part is approximately three or four typewritten pages in length. And the obliging magazine editor, more often than not, goes so far as to place a signalling white space between the parts.

Thus, the normal story is a matter of some sixteen to twenty pages of typewritten copy, a standard total of approximately five thousand words. Some stories, of course, are much shorter than this, some are longer. But the proportions remain about the same, although let me emphasize here that these lengths are norms. They are not to be considered as rigid and inviolable. After having learned their use, if you consider you have good cause to alter the dimensions a bit, feel free to do so.

Part 1: The Situation.
In this section you must do the following:
  (a) state the problem, dynamically and subjectively;
  (b) introduce and characterize *all* the significant characters, if not in person, at least by mention or plain implication;
  (c) set the stage, clearly indicating time, place and circumstances.

Stating the problem dynamically and subjectively means, as a general principle, giving the so-called *narrative hook*. The narrative hook is the first brief, potent statement of what is the matter with the central character, what his problem is, what difficulty he is facing. "And it came to pass after these things that *God did tempt Abraham*," to go back to our familiar example.

Think of this hook as a question mark. It snags the reader, who is always interested in other people's difficulties, always willing to make them, at least vicariously, his own. Have you ever observed how fast a crowd gathers about an accident or a fight? Similarly, your job is to catch that reader: strike the hook home just as fast and as firmly as you possibly can. Don't waste time upon it! Put the hook in the first sentence, or as soon thereafter as you can.

With the bitterness of death in his heart, Don Dashaway stared a long moment, then turned away.

That is an example, a rather crude one, of course, but look at it. Can you see how it fairly bristles with question hooks? What is this fellow so desperately bitter about? What is he staring at? If he is so bitter, why can't he do something about it; or is he starting to do something? Moreover, we have introduced a character and established him as the VP (since, obviously, only Don could be seeing the bitterness *inside* his own heart). All of this in one sentence.

Sometimes, of course, you can't slash right out like this and catch your fish on first cast. Sometimes you have to estimate the reader as more wary, or, perhaps, your bait is such that instant strikes are not possible. But in that case, like any other angler, you do a build-up—flick, flick, flick of the fly, until at last the reader is lured to strike. And you have him!

But, by all means, avoid deliberately trying *not* to hook your reader too speedily. If you can possibly get him on the first cast—first sentence—do it. And *never* state the problem objectively.

That fisherman catches few fish who conveys the objective truth to his quarry, clarifying for it the fact that what appeared mysterious and enticing is nothing more than a lure composed of chicken feathers, wood, sinew, dyes, and a concealed and exceedingly sharp hook. It is not done that way.

Introduce and characterize ALL *significant characters.*
Flatly and simply, this means what it says. In the first three or four pages you must bring in everybody who plays any significant part in your story. The hero, the heroine, the villain, the villainess, and all significant as-

sistants. Only the nameless spear bearers, the supernumeraries for the mob scenes, need not be included.

The reason is simple. In addition or subtraction of the arithmetical kind, you always set down all your factors first, before attempting the solution of the problem. You do precisely the same in story, thus preventing yourself from straying away from the problem at hand.

Characterization has already been discussed in Chapter III. But to do it as briefly and vividly as possible in this first section of your story, remember with John that "In the beginning was the Word." Use appropriate words for each character, appropriate physical descriptions, and, above all, appropriate small actions.

Thus a heroic character *never* whines, whimpers, cowers, sneers, jeers, quails, flinches; never is "utterly merciless" or brutal or craven or murderous or insolent or hard-hearted; never fails to smile at small children and dogs; never is described as "handsome, *but* with eyes just a little too close together"; never has a villainous sounding name.

It is for good reason that Hollywood renames Susie Glutze, making her Linda Lanier or something else with syllables equally sweet. You must do the same. Even though you may never have read the book, you know immediately that Uriah Heep, by the very sound of his name, is a villain, and David Copperfield a hero.

Do not omit the constant characterizing emphasis in your character-contradiction couples and tags and actions. Put the emphasis on the "good," the heroic, aspect of the heroic characters, and on the bad of the villains. Thus, "He was hideously ugly—until you got to know him," obviously describes by emphasis a heroic character, a Lincoln. But, "He was handsome—until you got to know him," quite as plainly describes a villain. "Her plain little face lighted up gloriously." That is a good charac-

ter. "Something unpleasant slithered across his mouth."
That is a villain. And so on.

If you cause your subjective drive to move briskly
from the outset, nearly all of this characterization technique will come naturally. Objectively, as I have described it here, it is perhaps difficult to grasp, but that is all
the more reason for learning the subjective side of your
business.

*Set the stage, clearly indicating time, place, and cir-
cumstances.*

This is the most objective of all the necessities of Part I.
But here, also, you should try to be objective in a soothing-
ly subjective way. That is, put the emphasis on the subjective aspects rather than on the necessary objective ones.
Try to place them on the inside of your sentences, as you
would the bitter part of a pill. For examples, pro and con:

Very seldom does a story begin thus: "The time was
June, 1865, the place, San Antonio, Texas. Lee had sur-
rendered at Appomattox some three weeks previously.
Don Dashaway, who had been serving in Carter's Texas
Legion until the surrender, was walking across Alamo
Plaza when he saw his bitterest enemy, with whom he had
had a fight four years before." And so on.

Instead, applying and amplifying our elementary "bitterness in his heart" opening sentence, we have something
like this:

> With bitterness in his heart, Don Dashaway,
> ex-rebel, stared a long moment at his enemy, then
> turned away. From somewhere in the swarming,
> staring crowd of ragged riders came an explosive,
> astounded oath, and then another sound, a snicker.
> The shamed heat mounted to the taut flesh below his
> eyes, and Don Dashaway clenched his gaunt hands
> tight, looked blindly into space, and kept going.

You didn't do that in this warming, sullen, incredibly savage San Antonio of June, 1865. Swallow a sneering foe's open challenge, turn your back and run! With weapons in your belt! You didn't do it. Maybe the rest of the South had been beaten, had stopped fighting. But not Texas. Texans had won the last battle of the war. Texans were still grimly, bitterly ready to fight anybody at the drop of a ragged hat. And to show the white flag to a scalawag, to turn and stumble away through the bright sunlight of this plaza with its scores of amazed, outraged, furious eyes! You didn't, you couldn't—you stood instead and fought, to kill or to be killed. But Don Dashaway kept going.

In this example we have time, place, and some of the circumstances. And yet, not one of them is in the historical tense, properly speaking. We have placed them inside our narrative pills, keeping the emotional coating on the outside, so that they will be easy to swallow. Whether your story be a quiet domestic tale intended for the family trade, a literary story, or a violent action adventure, the method remains the same. Those who seek after facts, historical, scientific, or geographical, will find them in books whose purpose is something other than fictional.

In fiction, readers want fiction. The facts stand practically invisible. It becomes your task, therefore, to give the readers the facts in that fashion—do not insert anything about time, place, or circumstances that is not emotionally coated, that does not enhance the emotional conflict inherent in your story.

Finally, before leaving Part I, *make it a working rule to get your action in the present fully in operation before you stop to indulge in any extensive flashbacks.*

In other words, Don Dashaway, stumbling across the plaza, will be confronted by his outraged former company commander, who, with fire in his eye, will say, "Sergeant Dashaway, suh, I don't give two whoops in Halifax what yo' promised po' Tom McCullough. Nobody is goin' to disgrace Carter's Texas Legion as yo', suh, have just done. Eitheh yo' make that polecat, Hoskins, eat what he's just called us all or I'll not only see yo're blacklisted, suh, I'll take it personal."

After which dissertation, with its fishhook question, "Ah, and now what is Don going to do about that?" you can let Don stumble on, remembering bleakly in a brief flashback how he got into this situation in the first place—meaning, in the first paragraph.

Do not satisfy the reader's curiosity as to just how and why Don got himself on the spot where we found him in the first paragraph until you have aroused a still greater curiosity to learn the answer to, "Now what?" *Always ask a further and more dramatic question before answering the preceding one.*

You are most positively not trying to satisfy that reader's curiosity at this point in the story. Your purpose is to cause him to read the whole story before he is satisfied. This being so, do not tell him why Don is pitted against the villain before asking him, "And what do you think is going to happen, now that Don is all snarled up with his old commander, too?"

Let me repeat:

Flashback, which, incidentally, is the only correct, "story" way by which we can bring in what has happened before our story opens—i.e., why Don and the villain are at swords' points—is simply the VP character *remembering in the present* what has happened in the past. If you do not ignore the "remembering in the present" part, you will ordinarily handle your problem very well. But please note here that when Don does remember why he and the villainous Hoskins are at odds, Part 1 of the story is complete. You have given the full opening situation.

Yet you have not done so at the cost of losing the reader's interest. The editor may put a space break between parts 1 and 2, but actually, as far as the reader's interest is concerned, there is no break at all. We have linked parts 1 and 2 together, just like links of a chain, because the Captain's bluff ultimatum is a complication, and as such is a portion, at least, of Part 2. We have simply interlaced the end of Part 1 and the beginning of Part 2 to maintain suspense, just as you would have to do with successive links of a chain you intended to suspend somewhere.

Is it clear at this point that I am *not* saying that Part 1 always ends with a flashback? There is no rule governing the placement of flashback, unless it may be said that it must come in naturally; that is, only where the character would remember it. Many excellent stories have, properly speaking, no consciously written flashback at all; it is present, rather, by implication. But when you find it desirable to use flashback, as you often will in answering the opening question, be sure that you do not insert it until you have raised a further and more dramatic question. By this means you keep hold of the curiosity of the reader.

Part 2: The Complication.

The Captain's ultimatum was the first complication arising from our hero's decision and action at the beginning of our story. Plainly it was a complication. It was not part of the opening situation; instead, it arose out of the opening situation. But now that it has arisen, patently our Don must decide and act within the framework of a much more complicated and agonizing problem.

In the beginning, he had only his conscience set off against his pride. He could keep his word and not shoot it out with Hoskins, or, with stiff-necked pride, he could forget what he had promised Tom McCullough (about not shooting Hoskins, we will suppose) and let the villain have it, socko!

But now, since he did *not* shoot Hoskins and the Captain did see the affair, Don must either reverse himself and go back and fight Hoskins or face the enraged and beloved Captain. If he keeps his word to McCullough, he has a fight on his hands with the Captain. Now what is he going to do?

What you, the author, are going to do is load the situation upon him! Give him no mercy; get him in deeper and deeper and deeper. Bring up something to remind him poignantly of poor old Tom and how much Tom trusted his (Don's) word. Let him decide that his pledged word to Tom McCullough is still paramount, so that he must ride out of town—run, no matter what people think. Let him head for the livery barn and find there four of his former comrades, sent by the Captain to see that he does *not* run away. They will shoot him rather than let him run.

Now what to do? He can't kill the faithful four, merely in order to get away, can he? Yet he can't stay either. He goes back to plead his case with the Captain, which is still more complication. Here is the swaggering Hoskins contemptuously confronting Don again on the sidewalk, giving him until sundown to leave town or be horsewhipped out. What is Don going to do now?

Part 3: THE CRISIS.

Again the parts link. But this part must contain the supreme complication, the supreme moment of decision and action, and, generally, the black moment as well. To carry on with our simple example, the hero swallows even Hoskins' final insult, goes on to the Captain, tells him flatly that he is not going to go back on his pledge to Mc-Cullough and shoot it out with Hoskins. In a flat monotone, the Captain says, "All right. Get out!" *But,* as Don mounts his horse to flee, one of his former mates comes to tell him bitterly that the Captain is taking the quarrel upon his own shoulders.

The beloved Captain, with a bullet crippled arm, is going to face Hoskins in Don's stead. The Captain is going to uphold the honor of the old command. And the Captain hasn't one chance in a thousand against that ace gunfighter.

Now what does Don do?

Here he stands, confronted with his supreme decision, the crisis of the whole story. And (this is worth reading several times) *in all probability he will now make his decision just as such supreme decisions actually are made in real life.* He will act, I mean, *in character, subconsciously, in accord with his fundamental make-up.*

He will act first and only later realize why he acted as he did. This is how you fall in love or make any of the other supreme decisions of life! The reasons for the decision are realized only after the incarnating decision and action, and not before.

Don will start back, thinking he means to protest violently again to the Captain. On the way he will sight Hoskins once more, just as the Captain is coming across the street. No further room for delay! Either Don must act or the Captain will, *right now.* And it is sundown, too, the deadline instant. So Don moves forward and flings into the villain's face the challenge, "All right, Hoskins. It's sundown and here I am. If it's fight you're craving, cut yourself a slice. I'm coming at you."

Face set, he goes for the fellow in a steady, even stride, and the die is cast, the decision made, the incarnating action begun.

Let us stop to analyze it, as Don *does not*. The decision has been based on a sudden, instinctive, and final grasping of all the facets of the now completely complicated situation. Don cannot run away. That, almost certainly, would bring death to the Captain and disgrace to the gray command to which both the Captain and Don had belonged. Don cannot shoot Hoskins. That would break his pledge to his dead partner, Tom McCullough. *But*, he *can* walk straight into Hoskins' fire and die.

That course would at least be honorable, and it would satisfy the grim Captain and the other members of the old command. This, remember, is not their personal quarrel. Veterans of four years of war, one human life means little to them now. But honor, in life or death—that is different.

Not *whether* a man lives or dies, but *how* he does it is what matters to them and to Don, as well. So . . .

Walking straight into Hoskins' fire does not mean shooting him. Don's promise is not being broken so long as Don himself does not fire.

So he marches straight toward the cursing killer, gaunt face set, eyes slitted, arms swinging. The black moment! And in that swift, pregnant instant we come to

Part 4: THE CLIMAX, ANSWER, OR "REWARD."
What happens? Consider the crouching villain a moment as he faces the oncoming Don. The would-be killer has seen these grim, gray fighting men come on just so against a foe, perhaps a foe with overwhelming superiority. And yet they came on, and, more often than not, conquered! He knows that, and, further, he is desperately uneasy, afraid.

Inside, he knows that he is wrong in this affair—he is playing the villain's part. No man can be brave in a situation in which he cannot justify himself to himself. And the sudden silence, the cold hostility of all those staring eyes. But, above all, the set purpose of that merciless on-coming figure. Step, step, step . . .

What would you do if you did not know that this charging warrior had no intention of shooting, but, instead, expected him to explode in lightning, deadly speed, and gun flame at any second?

Right! Hoskins' face goes gray. He tries to draw his gun. Something, the whirling spindrift of terror that goes before a charge, perhaps, or the cloud front before a hurricane, catches him in its giant grip, spins him about. And he's running!

Running away, broken, disgraced, as destroyed in this bleak San Antonio of 1865 as though he were dead and buried. And Don has his reward, his answer.

By deciding and moving to sacrifice his own life for honor's sake, he has preserved both his honor and his life. He has kept his promise to McCullough, saved the Captain from probable death, and retained his self-respect and the respect of his comrades, as well. Aside from saving his own life, he has destroyed a villain.

For the supreme sacrifice, the supreme reward.

And we have caused something to happen fictionally that has happened in real life time and again. "One riot—one Ranger!" It was not just a fictional invention in the Texas of those days, nor yet in the roaring decades afterwards, when the West we now know only in fiction was fact. Time and again lone fighting men, Texas Rangers, marshals, gun fighters, outfaced would-be killers, even mobs of them, and compelled them to surrender or turn and run. And they often accomplished their purpose without touching a gun. It is not fiction, for it happened; and here in our fictional version, if we are sufficiently capable, we make that breathless moment live again.

To recapitulate briefly:

Part 1, *Situation:* State the problem, introduce *all* the significant characters, set the stage.

Part 2, *Complication:* Confront the central character with the further and more dramatic problems arising from his initial decision and action. Bring the other characters against him like the blockers and tacklers in a football game, the blockers trying to help, the tacklers trying to pull him down. Test and test again, and make each problem more difficult than the one that preceded it. And each time the central character must decide and act speedily.

Part 3, *Crisis:* The central character comes to the supreme test, the last and most deadly tackler of all. Now it's make or break. He makes and acts on the supreme decision, which apparently is going to cost him all. He drives through the black moment and—

Part 4, *Climax:* He arrives at his reward, his goal. The supreme gift for the supreme sacrifice. This reward is placed at the end of the blind trail of righteousness by you, the creator. The hero does not know that it is waiting there. He simply has faith, whereas you, the author, who tossed him in there:

"*. . . He that toss'd Thee down into the Field*
He *knows about it all—*HE *knows—*HE *knows!*"

For the 1 — 1 version, simply note the decisions and actions of Hoskins, the villain.

And that is all there is to story parts.

One final thrust now at the positive nature of the supreme decision and action, and we are done. I have said this before, in different words, but again: the decision and action can be negative in form, but always they must be positive in inner force, in content.

The hero's decision in our story is an example. He decides *not* to shoot the villain and does *not* shoot him. But consider how hard a decision it is to live by, how much will power the hero must use in accomplishing it. Do not let the common definition of negative, i.e., something weak or lacking, lead you into error here. Make even the negative decisions difficult ones, difficult to fulfill.

In tales intended for feminine audiences the difficult negative decision is very often used. The virtuous heroine, for example, realizing that she has fallen madly in love with the fiancé of her best friend, will decide *not* to marry him, even though she is certain she can. This is always a desperately hard decision to make, even though it is negative; in each case, it apparently will "break her heart forever" or "ruin her life." But she makes the decision nevertheless, and incarnates it by going away—to be duly rewarded by the discovery that her friend is already married to somebody else (or loves somebody else), that the young man loves only her (the heroine, of course!), and, further, that, had she selfishly tried to get him, she most assuredly would have lost him, because he likes unselfish young ladies best. How many times have we read it!

Ordinarily, in accord with their different natures, a man in a man's story must act positively, by displaying both faith and works, whereas a woman need show only faith. (Nowadays, however, it will do no harm to let the woman produce a few good, confirming works for the sake of women's rights.) Either way, faith alone or faith with works, it is always the hard choice, not the easy, the strong, not the weak, that produces story and acceptances.

And there are no accidents in story. You, as author, must see to it that they never occur. Even those happenings that look like accidents to the characters involved always occur in strict accord with the author's plan. In the story you are the creator and master of all you survey.

V

The Finishing Touches

Seek ye first the kingdom . . . and all these
things shall be added.

MATTHEW, 6:33

THE other thirty-seven chapters usually to be found
in a book on writing will be condensed, without loss
of flavor or essential vitamins, I hope, in this chapter.
And you need not read it at all unless you chance to need
the specific information it contains.

This chapter will cover, then, slanting to markets,
choice of markets, preparing manuscript for submission,
the novelette, the magazine novel, working habits, how to
get yourself off dead center, copyright, the scene, style
(if any), pointers, tags—everything that I may not have
covered, or, at any rate, may not have covered clearly in
the preceding chapters.

Working backwards, through the list, we consider
first:

Tags and Pointers.

If you have done a good job of getting the subjective
element into your story, putting the "Me" in vividly, then
tags and pointers—for example, the all-important pre-
dominant direction of your sentences—will come automatically. Essentially they are the shape of things to come,
the "future" aspects of events, including their signs in
the present. But, to speak of them objectively for purposes of clarity:

Pointers are your intangible straws pointing the wind. Usually they are significant statements or actions by the character involved—just how significant, we learn in retrospect, of course. Thus, Abraham *points* quite clearly when, at the beginning of Genesis 22, our prime example of the 1 + 1 story, he answers the Lord, "Here I am." He *answers* when the Lord calls, and at once. So, intuitively, we expect that, when the Lord calls again, at the directed place and moment of sacrifice, Abraham will be there, obeying, ready to answer as before, "Here I am."

We are not surprised at his being there, *because the pointer subtly told us that was the way the story was going.*

"Speak of the devil," is a phrase by which we cheerfully recognize a pointer when someone of whom we were just speaking appears on the scene. By one means or another, that is about what you do to evoke your devil or heroine, and also to forecast his or her probable actions. "Coming events cast their shadow before," is still another time-honored phrase in which this principle is recognized. And the technical device itself is by no means hard to master.

Simply look the right way—forward, that is—and let your character be casually natural about it. Thus, if your cowboy character is to participate in a scene in town near the middle of your story, what more natural than for him to note, in the early part, that Saturday is pay day, or that he is nearly out of tobacco, or that he has to see the banker about a mortgage within the next day or two.

If he is going to shoot somebody, let him worry a little about the possibility of "trouble" should he and the villain chance to meet. If he is going to "just happen" to meet the heroine, let him rather hope he will, remembering that sometimes she, too, goes to town on Saturday. And so on and so on. And, as I have already said, if you have mastered the correct, subjective way of looking at your story, all of this comes as naturally and as effortlessly as looking up the street and seeing what lies in that direction, instead of looking down the street and trying to tell what is behind you. It is merely a matter of which direction you choose to look.

Plants are ordinarily physical objects, but sometimes they are facts, persons, motives, or conditions needed in the story and *of whose existence the reader must be informed in advance.*

They are much like pointers, in other words, save that they are more objective. Hence, while you can materialize an action on, say, page 14 and let its intangible shadow, its pointer, appear as early as page 3, plainly a hard material object, a horse pistol, for example, is a horse pistol of another color. If you need the horse pistol on page 14, you cannot very well have its ghost appearing on page 4; it does not have a ghost; nor can you materialize it quite unexpectedly from nothing whatever when you need it. That would look too much like accident; and let me emphasize again, *no genuine, unforeseen accidents ever take place in story.*

Happenings that may appear accidental to the VP character and others in the story may occur, yes. But you, the creator, know what is going to happen. It is all according to plan. *And you must contrive to give your reader also some part of this superior awareness.*

Thus, to get the horse pistol into the picture according to plan, and not by sheer accident, on page 14, you must have the heroine open the table drawer on page 4, when she is looking for a pencil or something else, and cause her to shudder a little at the sight of Pop's old army pistol in there.

That is all. The little shudder looks very casual and meaningless. But when, on page 14, the heroine needs a horse pistol badly in order to defend her honor or some-thing else precious to her, we are not in the least surprised that she gets one out of the same drawer. We knew it was there all along; moreover, we sensed it was there for a purpose.

Even a grand piano needs planting—if the heroine is going to push it over on the villain. Similarly, if a gangster is going to tell Mama that her erring daughter is about to get into trouble (I am taking this from a "slick magazine" story recently published), plant the gangster several pages earlier. Have Mama casually notice him somewhere. It will look very casual until the gangster comes in with the all-important information. But when he does, the reader will not be unduly surprised. Having been planted pre-viously (as all gangsters should be), this character creates no exasperating accident later. By the same token, you, as author, have pleased your cash customers, the readers.

Never put your reader in the position of having to ask impatiently, "Why doesn't the author *tell* us these things?" when anything of importance happens in your story. Point to significant actions. *Plant* all of the objects, facts, persons, and conditions that you are going to need. If a valuable vase is going to be broken on page 15 by a careless maid, then plant the thing early—on page 6 have the heroine dust it carefully and remember with a loving sigh who gave it to her.

In short, look the right way, up the street, not down, and see things coming.

Tags.

These are simply the "signs" of character. They offer a swift, sharply focussed method of presenting as com-plete a picture as possible of your character each and every time he enters the story.

Thus, teeth and glasses were Theodore Roosevelt's appearance tags. Using such a Rooseveltian character, we would spotlight the teeth and glasses every time he came on the stage. "His strong, white teeth gleamed." "Setting his glasses more firmly on his nose, he picked up the paper and ground his teeth." " 'Bully!' he cried, his eyes twinkling behind their thick lenses." And so on.

Tags may be of appearance, as with T.R.'s teeth and glasses; of expression, of mannerism, or even of habit of thought—a character might be very, very sad in everything he said, for example, and that would be a tag. "Bully!" neatly tags T.R. by expression, for it was one of his favorite exclamations. "My friends," similarly tags Franklin D. Roosevelt. Both Roosevelts carry the habit of vigorous, direct thought. Like the identification tags, or the collar insignia of soldiers, these story tags serve to identify the wearers anywhere and keep them separated in the minds of readers.

It is good practice to use at least two different kinds of tags, e. g., of appearance and of mannerism, or of appearance and habit of thought, for all significant characters. For your principal characters, use tags in all four classes if you can, and *don't forget that these tags should come in pairs symbolizing the emotional conflict that creates the character.*

T.R.'s glasses (the resistance) and his strong teeth (the force), for example. Franklin D. Roosevelt's clear, strong voice (the force) and his halting gait or necessity for remaining seated (the resistance). It is not nearly so hard to symbolize such character-creating, positive-negative conflicts as you might imagine. Try it! Try tagging the people you know, the ones you meet, until it becomes a habit. And note, too, how easy it is to recognize the tags of the truly superior characters.

The Basic Formulas of Fiction

The Scene.

Much beloved by analysts of fiction from Aristotle to today's critics, the *scene* is a static unit of drama, a sort of formal molecule, derived, of course, from the drama, in which the formal handling of the VP is necessary.

In the correct scene, as in the correct story, there is always an *opening situation*, a *conflict* of opposing emotional forces, a *plot decision*, or "break" (remember Omar Khayyam's ball?), and an *answer*, or result. Into which *answer* (and once again, as in a complete story by gross parts) is interlaced the advance elements of a *sequel*. An excellent exposition of this fundamental building stone of story can be found in *Writing Magazine Fiction*, by Walter S. Campbell.[1]

Yet, perversely perhaps, I choose to differ with my great friend, mentor, and superior on the importance of knowing all about even the embryo of your story. I think that it is something the dramatist and the screen or radio writer assuredly should know. But I doubt its value for the author of fiction.

The rigid arrangement of the VP trinity in the theater obviously makes scenes necessary. The audience will be seated out front, the central character will be on the stage, and the author, we presume, can be found playing Trembling Hope amongst the choir invisible in, if not on, the wings. At regular intervals the curtains must be dropped and the audience left to its own private viewpoints while the actors change and perspiring stalwarts reset the stage. But you have none of these static divisions to contend with in the written story.

Instead, if you have worked correctly, you have but one continuing scene, involving the combined "Me" of yourself, your VP character, and your reader. No formal

[1] Garden City, Doubleday, Doran & Co., 1940.

98

seating arrangements divides these three, or even any two of them, which is one reason for the fact that moving pictures have approached, but never quite attained, the perfect continuity of the written story. Author, character, reader—all are one in the good written story, and you have no real intermissions, no breaks.

Even your time and space transitions are leaped by your moving tripartite "Me" at lightning speed and without a second's hesitation. Even physically, you are closer to your audience than in any other medium.

The stage actor is across the pit and footlights, the screen star is a shadow, the radio performer a ghost in the fathomless void. But you have your story precisely in your reader's hands, in physical contact with him, not three feet away from his nose. Moreover, he need not comply with any particular formalities in order to read. He need not sit in a theater seat, or turn on and tune in at the scheduled second. He can carry your story with him and read wherever there is enough light. He can start, stop, start again, at his own convenience. It seems to me that a writer is foolish if he does not take every advantage of this intimacy; and I cannot see that he does take advantage when he encumbers himself with the limitations of other fields of story telling, the stage-scene division particularly.

Yet, if you chance to have a mind inclined to soar entirely away from objectivity and lose itself in pure subjective wandering, the discipline of scene writing may help. Scene writing is part of the basic course requirement in the fiction writing classes at the University of Oklahoma, where I teach. In the advanced courses, in which complete stories are attempted, it has been my experience thus far that some writers are considerably helped by breaking their plots into scenes, while others can't seem to do it at all. Perhaps it is a matter of personal taste and inclination.

Fictional Sentences.

Some years of sad experience persuade me either that I can't say this clearly or that I don't emphasize it enough in the average case. If you do not need this encore, please forgive me. The fictional sentence has its power, its drive, concentrated on the feeling, the emotional, the *forward-looking* part of the sentence. And if most of your sentences do not run thus, you are probably not writing fiction.

On a typical typewritten page of fiction there will be, say, fifteen sentences. Eight or nine of them, possibly even more, will start with the emotion. "Agonizedly, he turned." "Hands clenching, he moved away." "An angry light glowed in the general's eye and . . ." "Fury drove him forward." And so on.

These are simplifications, of course, and are presented merely that you may see them. Genuine emotion is not any word or arrangement of words, but rather the author's subtle emphasis upon what he writes. Hence, in the smoother fiction copy, it is very difficult to see the emotion in the sentence beginnings, though it is easy enough to feel the cumulative effect. But the idea is to put this emphasis upon emotion at the beginning of the majority of your sentences, no matter how you contrive to do it.

The other sentences will be straightaway, matter-of-fact affairs. "He walked away." "The man picked up the gun." "Turning, he moved toward the house." "She was small." And so on.

Some writers are able to get this emotional-drive effect without parading the feeling so, putting it up front like the flag in a procession. But most of us, and particularly beginners, are not so imbued with the subjective drive that we make it unmistakable in everything we write. We have to use method, I mean; and *this is the easiest method.* Moreover, it is the best method I know for getting oneself off dead center.

Whenever you feel that your writing is going dead, or that something is wrong, check up on the subjective-objective direction first.

See whether you are writing fact or fiction. Are you starting a majority of your sentences with the subjective emotionals, the "feeling" flags? If you are not, go back and deliberately reverse the majority of your objective, straightaway sentences.

Make, "He whirled angrily," read instead, "Angrily, he whirled." "He turned, eyes slitted," becomes "Eyes suddenly slitted, he turned." And so on, putting in emotionals if they are not there, putting them in at the beginning of sentences.

Force yourself to do it. If you are on the deadest possible center, your first efforts at reversing probably will sound rather awful. But keep it up! In nine cases out of ten the results will be what you desire: you are in the fiction groove once more. Then, of course, go back and smooth up your sputtering start.

Perhaps another picture will do more than words. Here is that subjective-objective, fiction-looks-forward, fact-looks-backward wheel again. We want to make it go somewhere, spin out a story for us. Very well. On which side, the top or the bottom, will you push in order to make it go ahead?

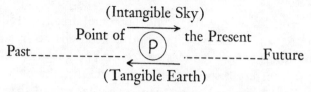

(Intangible Sky)

Point of ————▶ the Present

Past _ _ _ _ _ _ _ _ _ _ _ ◀—— _ _ _ _ _ _ _ _Future

(Tangible Earth)

Slanting and Style.

In just the reverse of the way most beginners try the trick, you *slant* a story objectively, but attain *style* subjectively. Thus, you escape being merely imitative. Moreover, you reduce the job from one that is hard intellectually to one that is hard in the same way that ditch digging is hard, no matter how shrewd you are about hefting a shovel.

To *slant* a story to a particular market or class of markets, notice first what kind of characters, scenery, plot action, and plot equation the magazines in this category prefer.

These are all objective aspects, please note, and amount to much the same thing. You then make up your story, having regard for these general factors.

For example, suppose you want to try one of the women's "slick" magazines. You read it and discover that the editors will take stories about middle-aged people sometimes but obviously prefer—they just love—yarns about young characters. These youngsters may or may not be married, but, oh, definitely, they are of the better class, their problems are not basically proletarian—they are typically a young married couple in a nice little home, have a car not too big or glossy (this is prewar, of course), and are possessed of social connections. And their problem is a social problem. "Shall Susabella spend the rainy-day fund to buy an expensive bridesmaid's gown for her society friend's wedding; or shall she swallow her pride and confess to the friend that she can't afford the dress now?"

You know the story and outcome already, needless to say, and even the story and central-character equation! *Marital love + social pride = ?* You know intuitively that, after all sorts of struggles, the little heroine will swallow her social pride, confess to her friend that she can't buy the dress—it would hurt hubby too much. Whereupon the friend will exclaim, "Why, naïve child! The dresses are paid for already, Auntie bought them. Come on down and have yours fitted."

That is a real story from a late issue of a leading woman's slick, by the way. Don't, therefore, steal it bodily. You can make up your story from similar materials. For example (plucking one from the air), you might write one about (1) a nice young doctor (2) engaged to a lovely youngster whose (3) very rich Aunt May doesn't like him one bit. Aunt May wants the girl to marry another man. Very well, (4) Aunt May gives a very fluff week-end party at her country home for the girl, and for the young doctor, too, of course. But (6) the young medico hasn't the proper clothes for such a society event and can't buy them unless he foregoes buying some surgical instruments he needs.

What happens? You know at once that he does *not* spend the money on white tie and tails, even though he has a quarrel with the girl about the matter and she announces defiantly that she is going anyway—alone. And the bitter rival, Aunt May's candidate, will be there, too, won't he? But our young M.D. buys the instruments and has his Black Moment. Then Aunt May's young hellion of a son, left to run wild during the party, strays off and breaks his neck. Because our young doctor is the only medical man available, he saves the boy, but *only* because he has the new instruments. Aunt May and the heroine fall upon his neck, loudly announcing that they realize now how wrong they were. Why, he's a wonderful man to have handy, and preferably with the proper surgical tools, rather than the requisite tails!

And that is our similar story. For a western magazine, you would go through the same procedure, doubtless discovering that the story must almost invariably revolve about a young cowboy involved in a violent controversy over cattle, range land, gold shipments, keeping a town law abiding, or something similar. Always there is a gunfight; there may be several; generally, nowadays, there

is love interest; and almost always the story equation is
$1 + 1$.

Make up your story from similar materials on the same general pattern. Don't send detective stories to the westerns, yarns about middle-aged people to the romantic love magazines, cowboy tales to the true confessions, or slambang gunplay to the sedate slicks. Give them each the kind of things—people and happenings—their readers want (or their editors think their readers want, rather, which isn't the same thing). That is about all there is to *slanting*.

It is much more sensible to slant to groups than to slant to individual magazines, since not infrequently a story may make several trips out before it is sold. Indeed, until you are an experienced writer, it is better still not to force this slanting process at all. By simple trial and error, you will find that you do one type of story better than you do others. This is your natural slant. If this is the case, concentrate on it and the magazines carrying similar material.

Perhaps just here it would be well to point out that few writers are naturally slanted for *The Saturday Evening Post* and nothing else; if this seems to be your only bent, you might do well to look again. It might be that you are only a glory hunter, rather than a writer. Ordinarily, even writers do not begin gloriously at the top and go up from there. (Sometimes when they do, the result is like a rocket fired from the top of Pike's Peak.) Slant pretty coldly and objectively, in other words, for what you think you can hit.

Style, on the contrary, is mainly a subjective quality, *not to be acquired by seeing and copying what other people do*. Your true *style* is not *what* you deal with, but *how* you deal with it. Nobody else can do anything precisely the way you can, nor can anybody else show you your best way.

When you try to copy another writer's style, you almost inevitably end up with a dead prettiness, a too-objectified way of writing which nobody will buy. Forget, then, the other fellow's way, his word arrangements, the objective aspects of his style, and try to make your writing more powerful, more vital and fast and punch-packed than his—*say it better than he does*. You may not develop a style better than his, but at least you will achieve a better one of your own.

This effort to be original, of course, can be overdone. There is no great objection to watching other writers and picking up little tricks and turns which you make your own. But be sure that you have made them your own, that you have digested and absorbed them and are using them as you should, *instinctively*. Do not forget that style is only superficially form: the words and word arrangements you can see. Fundamentally, style is force, the driving, efficient way in which you yourself, with your own peculiar character and limitations, apply the power inside you. It is a power which is yours alone to apply.

The Novelette.

Expand a short story by introducing more complications, more minor crises, more characters to compound into a correspondingly greater emotional explosion and recombination at the climax, and you have the modern magazine novelette. It will range in length from about nine thousand words (sometimes even shorter in the love pulps) to a maximum of about fifteen thousand.

Typically, there will be about five chapters, each two thousand to three thousand words long and each ending on a suspense note, very much like the movie installments of a serial. In the longer novelettes there may be two or three VP's, the changes taking place generally (but not always) between chapters. But, until you become very proficient in fiction writing, you will be on safest ground if you hold to one VP, even in a novelette. By this means you may be reasonably sure your story is not straying.

Anyone who has mastered the short-story form can quite readily expand a good plot into novelette length. But please note the prerequisite. A novelette is not achieved by leaving in all the dead wood, the useless words and incidents one would prune out of a short story. Nor, as a general rule, can a writer who does not know how to turn out salable short stories succeed in the novelette length.

A very common failing of beginners, invariably fatal, is the conviction, arrived at on page 16, that a short story is "turning out to be a good novelette." Which, of course, it isn't. The conviction occurs with such unvarying regularity, however, that one can lay down a rule. Here it is:

Always begin your novelettes on page 1 and at no other place.

Whenever a short story starts "turning out to be a novelette" on about page 15 or 20, always stop right there, check back, observe what a sloppy job of writing you have been doing, and cut mercilessly to get within short-story space tolerances. Not one time in one hundred will a fat, flabby short story, masquerading as a novelette, get by the editorial eye.

When you do *set out* to write a novelette, time your story to have a peak of dramatic, emotional action about every three or four pages. In the action pulps, this peak will be a fight, a robbery, a flight, a showdown, or something of the kind. In the more restrained markets, it will not be so violently physical, but it will be even stronger on the emotional side. *Do not omit these peaks.*

Moreover, do not try to run the peaks together. You cannot do it, of course, but if you could, your story all peak would be as flat and monotonous as one all valley.

To be interesting, a story should roll, like rolling country, with an always changing variety of hills and vales, peaks and depressions. And your *story timing*, or pace, incidentally, is most easily measured from peak to peak, wave top to wave top.

In its pace, or timing, the novelette is only slightly slower than the short story, in which time, literally, must take off and fly.

Most novelettes adhere to one story thread. A few develop two, or even three. In any event, the slightly more leisurely timing permits you to develop your various storm elements more completely—that is, you can tell more of the villain's emotional conflict, more of the heroine's, more of the other characters', thus making them all more alive and potent at your final climactic decision and action.

The Magazine Novel.

This varies in different magazines from about ten thousand to as many as fifty thousand words, the average being about twenty thousand. In the shorter lengths, the magazine novel more nearly resembles the novelette; in the longer ones, it reaches the serial. Its typical requirements are about the same as those of the novelette, the chief difference being the matter of timing. Whereas the short story is the fastest of all, the "complete novel" is the slowest of "all-in-this-issue" fiction, being exceeded in leisureliness only by the serial and the genuine book novel.

Incidentally, the matter of the speed of a story is itself highly interesting. If we are to judge from students passing through our laboratory, most beginning writers already are "timed" by something innate. About one out of every twenty writes at novel speed; the rest are either of short-story tempo or nothing. Apparently it is possible in some cases to change from a kind of natural novel timing to short-story timing, or vice versa, without fatal results;

and some are seemingly equipped by nature for two-speed performance. But find out for yourself whether you are the persevering tortoise or the sprint-star hare! Usually it is best to put one's best foot forward!

For the magazine novel, these salient points, which apply also, in still greater degree, to the magazine serial:

(1) Since a magazine novel or serial must be strong enough to be featured on the cover, indeed, must often "carry the issue," it is usually harder to sell than a short story. It is a different matter, of course, if one has already achieved an established name. But the typical progress of a new writer is from short stories, to novelettes, then, finally, to novels.

(2) Loosely, the magazine novel has the same general structure and plot pattern as the short story. You will nearly always find that a novel could be boiled down to a short story. But, in so doing, you would lose all of the interesting build-up and compounding of the minor characters—difficult matter to write interestingly, but absorbing if it is well done. In a novel, you tell the whole story of your central character and a great deal of the story of the other significant characters, whereas, in a short story, you epitomize the hero and hardly more than label the others.

(3) Book novels, studies of character without illustrating problems, progressions from something to nothing, or sequences of events strung meaninglessly together almost never can be sold to a magazine. Unless, of course, one is a flagpole sitter, trans-Atlantic flier, president's wife, or someone similarly qualified by well-publicized contradiction. If you intend to sell your story as a magazine novel or serial, *plot it* and fill it with dramatic action. There is always a market, and sometimes a surprisingly good one, for the plotted action story. Repeatedly stories of this type, intended for the pulps, have sold to the very highest-paying "slick" magazines.

The Finishing Touches

Preparing Your Manuscript for Market.

The rules here are simple and explicit:

(1) Use an excellent grade of white bond paper, plus cleaned type and a fresh ribbon on your typewriter.

(2) Put your name and address in the extreme upper left-hand corner of your first page. In the upper right-hand corner put the word count of your story, and, if necessary, a brief indication of what you are offering. Thus:

> Approximately 5,000 words
> Usual rates

Make your word count in round numbers; that is, 4,000, 4,250, 4,500, and so on. To set down 3,672.4 words is the mark of an amateur. Do not offer your manuscript at cut rates. Since stories must sell the magazine, the editor would be stupid if he bought anything save first-rate merchandise. As a general rule put nothing at all below the word count.

However, if you must ask a higher rate than that you know the market ordinarily pays, this is the time and place to say so. This is the time and place also to reserve whatever rights you think you had better hold back. (See section on *Rights* later in this chapter.) But, for the beginner, it is the part of discretion not to say anything here. Let the editor buy what he wants until you are in a position to bargain with him.

(3) Next, turn down approximately one-third of the first page and in the center write your story title, with your name or pen name immediately below, like this:

DON DASHAWAY'S DESPERATION
By John Jones

109

(4) Give yourself another inch and one-half of white space and begin your story, leaving generous margins on both sides. Leave space at the bottom, too.

(5) On succeeding pages repeat the story title in the extreme upper right-hand corner, followed by the page number. Thus:

Don Dashaway's Desperation . . . 2

(6) Do not divide words at the ends of lines. If you can write but half of the word at the end of the line, leave blank space instead and put the whole word on the next line. Reason: printers have a habit of following copy literally and consequently may hyphenate a word in the middle of a line of type.

(7) At the end of your story, put some # # # to indicate the close and repeat your name and address, just in case page 1 is lost.

(8) Do *not* permanently bind your manuscript. It may be mailed with pages unbound to most markets. However, it is better to bind it in an attractive cover, using the paper staples normally obtainable in any stationery store, the kind that can be unfastened with the fingers. Better still, use one of the manuscript covers costing about 5 cents which can be found on nearly all stationery counters. *This cover, remember, is the packaging of your product; make it is neat and attractive as you possibly can.*

(9) Mail flat. Do not roll. Use a large kraft envelope with a slightly smaller size for the return of manuscript—say, 10 x 13 inches and 9½ x 12½, respectively. Address both envelopes, the larger to The Editors of the magazine to which you are submitting, the smaller to yourself. Put the return envelope and manuscript into the larger envelope, have it weighed at the post office (it must be sent by first-class post), and *stick the return postage on the return envelope yourself.* This last may spare you the ex-

pense of paying all but 3 cents of the return postage a second time. Loose stamps are sometimes lost in the shuffle of manuscript handling in editorial offices.

(10) It is not at all necessary to include a letter. Most magazine editors are intelligent enough to know why you sent the manuscript. But, if you must write, make it brief. Two or three paragraphs, say. If your story is based on unusual facts, or you are an expert in the field to which the story pertains—for example, if you have written a flying story after serving two years in the R.A.F.—tell the editor about it. It is very likely to help you make a sale.

(11) Is it necessary to add that you should keep *a carbon copy of your story and a record of where it went and when?*

Rights and Copyright.

There are so many rights involved even in the sale of a short story—first serial rights, second serial rights, book rights, movie rights, radio rights, foreign rights, and still others—that a large book could be written on the topic. Indeed, several have been. But, for the beginning writer, the solution can be summed in a sentence.

Submit only to reliable markets and wait until you become reasonably well known before standing up and loudly demanding all of your "rights." For a little fellow, prudence pays.

Many magazines nowadays, particularly in the pulp field, insist upon buying all rights. They have a very good reason for this, the reprint menace. Next to being imposed upon by an outright plagiarist, nothing maddens a magazine editor more than to find in a competing magazine a story he has bought and published previously. This is the reprinted story which appears a second time because the first editor did not insist upon the acquisition of all rights and the misguided author thought more of the few dollars the reprint publisher offered than of his own reputation. Don't ever be guilty of this kind of stupidity.

Ordinarily, the magazine editor will object not at all to newspaper syndication, radio, movie, book, or foreign re-use of the story he has bought from you and published. These markets are not direct competitors, and I myself have never had the least trouble in getting such rights cheerfully assigned to me. But second serial or reprint rights—that is, the right to sell the same story for one-tenth as much as was originally received for it to a directly competing magazine—Writer, do not ask it!

Sadly, some magazines may reprint their own stories, paying you nothing at all for thus profiting twice from your work. But you can easily find out which houses do this and avoid them. If you must withhold rights, even at the risk of losing a sale, make your position clear under the word count on the first page.

Write, "First American serial rights only," for example, if you wish to hold back everything else, including the privilege of translating into the Scandinavian. Or, "Radio rights withheld;" or, "Motion picture rights withheld," although it is generally a waste of time to worry about the movie possibilities of short fiction. Scarcely one short story in a thousand contains enough material for a movie. Or write—but again, the best course is not to write anything at all, but, instead, let the editor decide what he wants to buy. This, until you are well-established enough to set terms which under other circumstances could not be considered.

Even then, it is better to find a good agent and let him handle your assorted and bewildering rights. Only after years of work in his craft can a writer handle all of his own rights as satisfactorily as an expert agent. Literary rights are primarily a legal matter, and here, as in other aspects of the law, the layman who would plead his own case usually finds he has a fool for a client.

But in the matter of statutory copyright, at least, the fundamentals should be known even to the beginning writer.

You do not have to copyright your material in manuscript form; as a matter of fact, copyright registration of fiction cannot be secured until publication has occurred. You have a common-law right in anything you produce, just as you have in other possessions. If the material contained in a manuscript story is stolen from you, you may proceed against the thief quite as you would if he had stolen your pig or your pocketbook. Hence, in submitting manuscripts to editors, you need take no unusual precautions, save to make reasonably sure beforehand that the market you choose is a reliable one.

Even if an editor should attempt to steal your story, it is much more likely that he would publish it under your name and forget to pay you for it than it is that he would lift it bodily and publish it under somebody else's name. The first course would ordinarily make him liable to civil court action for the collection of a debt; the second, however, would be much more serious for him, inasmuch as criminal proceedings would be involved.

Statutory copyright, under the United States Copyright Act of 1909 and the amendments thereto, is intended to give relief, but, as with most legal remedies, it is fairly complicated. Briefly, however, the act itself provides that the copyright proprietor (whether author or publisher, depending upon the nature of the prior agreement between the two) shall be protected in his ownership of the material published with notice of copyright for a period of twenty-eight years in the first instance. At the end of such period, copyright may be renewed for a further twenty-eight years by the author only, or by the author's widow, widower, or children, if separate copyright registration has been secured in the first instance for the short story in a magazine, let us say. If copyright has been secured for the contents of the composite work (magazine) by the publisher, then the publisher, not the author, may renew.

If the author wishes to secure copyright registration of a short story in a magazine, he must arrange with the publisher in advance of publication to print notice of separate copyright in the issue of the magazine in which the story appears. Promptly *after* publication with notice of copyright, the author must file with the Register of Copyrights, Library of Congress, Washington, D. C., the appropriate application form for copyright registration, together with fee of 2 dollars and one complete copy of the best edition of the periodical in question. If the publisher secures copyright in his own name, which is customary, he will do so for the magazine as a whole according to procedures very much like the above.

From a legal standpoint, as well as from the standpoint of practical advantage, it does not make a great deal of difference whether the author or publisher achieves copyright proprietorship. This is particularly true in relation to books. The contract between author and publisher precedes publication (and, therefore, copyright registration) and is presumed to give to each an equitable interest in publication. If the publisher, by contract, is given the privilege of taking out copyright, then he stands in the relation of trustee to the author in all matters which may impinge upon the rights guarded by copyright. The same may be said of the author if he, by contract, becomes copyright proprietor.

It is unlikely that a publisher who is not copyright proprietor of a given work will be any less zealous in safeguarding it from infringement, let us say, than the author-proprietor would be—for the reason that the publisher has a heavy investment in publication. On the other hand, a publisher is often better qualified than the author to deal with routine matters involving copyright: requests for permission to reprint, for example.

When a given copyright is infringed, the injured party may seek damages through legal action. You must be very sure, however, of infringement before you resort to legal redress. My advice is, always consult a lawyer. You cannot copyright subject matter: adventure, oil field life, romance, for examples. If another author uses your words and situations however, your lawyer will probably tell you that you have a case. Titles are not subject to copyright, but there are a number of interesting cases in which the fair-trade acts have been invoked to protect the first user of the title against unfair competition.

Markets.

Too many writers—and not necessarily beginning ones —fail to pay attention to market requirements and the wheres, hows, and whys of selling stories. One of the first duties of the professional writer is to think of his market before he starts to write. Moreover, it is well if he does not think inevitably and exclusively of *The Saturday Evening Post*. He should know that two-thirds of the full-time, professional fiction writers launch their careers in the so-called pulp magazines, in the little periodicals, or in the newspaper syndicates. Most writers begin modestly and work up in their profession.

It is pleasant, of course, to start at the top, but it is an infrequent experience. If we regard it as normal that the occupants of other professions—law, medicine, and engineering—must learn and gain experience before becoming expert, we can be sure that the same principle applies to the craft of writing. You will do well, therefore, to hitch your wagon to a work horse at first. Choose markets that you think you can achieve and try, try, try.

Markets, no less than the art of writing for them, must be studied. An intelligent writer will haunt the newsstands, just as a doctor devotes himself to a hospital, or a lawyer to the courthouse. The intelligent writer will have a specialty, even as most doctors and lawyers have. He will know all of the magazines in his own field, he will know the work of the better writers who appear in them, and he will read these magazines and authors regularly, not for entertainment but for business.

From his reading, he will know what the magazines are buying, whether the ones in which he is particularly interested are currently in the market, what the current rates are, the names of editors. He will get additional information from editors' letters and from writers' magazines, which will prove to be as valuable tools of his trade as his typewriter.

The Author & Journalist, a writers' magazine published in Denver, Colorado, and available on good newsstands almost everywhere, carries a quarterly market list of nearly all American and Canadian periodicals which buy fiction, poetry, and/or articles. Rates, addresses, current requirements, and even the speed with which a given market pays the author are given. This list will be found to be very satisfactory as well as inexpensive. The same magazine also carries a directory of book publishers annually which is equally satisfactory.

Writer's Yearbook, published by *Writer's Digest* at Cincinnati, Ohio, is a periodical usually to be found also on good newsstands, especially in the spring, when it is issued. This publication contains useful information on photograph and verse markets and syndicates, as well as the standard lists of periodical and book publishers. Ordinarily these lists are not quite so complete as the separate listings in *Author & Journalist*, but they are usually quite satisfactory.

The publishers of *Writer's Digest* also offer the most complete of all market listings, *The Writer's Market*, a cloth-bound book which covers practically every purchasing market an American writer ever heard of. Constantly revised, this book is somewhat expensive, but it is highly important to have on hand when you want to know where to send a story that may present unusual marketing problems.

In addition to these and other lists issued by various writing publications, the writers' trade magazines, *Writer's Digest*, *Author & Journalist*, *The Writer*, *Writers' Journal*, etc., all normally carry a number of interesting and often valuable market tips in each issue.

Agents.

"Shall I use an agent or shall I try to sell by mail to the editors?" I wish I knew the answer to this question!

Many writers seem to be able to work only through an agent. Others can't work with one. There is no rule of thumb. An agent who knows his business is like any other professional man: he can, and does, perform an important function.

Selling to pulps, however, is probably easier to do direct, providing you have persistence and sales ability. I once polled a number of leading pulp-magazine editors on the question. Three-fourths of them replied frankly that they preferred—some very much preferred—to deal direct with the writer, to make suggestions direct to him, and to build a friendship that would prove mutually profitable.

It is often true that an editor with whom you have a personal friendship, even if it is based upon nothing more than correspondence, will tip the balance in your direction on a doubtful story and send you a check. The same story, if submitted through an agent, might very well draw a rejection. After all, we tend to favor our friends; if an editor likes an agent, he can always buy somebody else's story from that agent.

Atop that, I doubt that the pulp editor ever lived who did not want to "discover" at least one new writing star, a new Sabatini, Kelland, Forester, Nason, Baldwin, or Norris. If the agent finds you first, the editor is only a second-hand discoverer. But, on the other hand, what a truly good agent can do for you!

Slick magazine sales, for example. From this distance, it appears that about 75 per cent of what the big slick-magazine editors buy is actually sold to, rather than bought by, them. In our own laboratory work here at the University of Oklahoma, we find that at least three-fourths of our pulp sales are made direct to editors, but nine-tenths of the slick sales are made by agents.

This becomes quite understandable when it is realized that the beginner's word rate at present may be as little as half a cent, or even less, whereas the writer for a slick magazine may get 10 cents a word and up for a story sometimes no better. Working for a typical 10 per cent commission, the agent may find himself faced with a much harder job when he is selling for the beginner and earning a magnificent $2.50 for his own part than when he is selling for a "name writer" to a slick. What would you do if you were in the agent's shoes?

Summed up, this means that it is very difficult for a rank beginner to acquire a good agent. Until a beginner has made three or four sales on his own, thus demonstrating that he has some ability, at least, the legitimate agent can scarcely afford to devote time to him. Literary agents, like other professional people, are in business to make money—which they cannot do by endlessly coaching beginners more or less "for free." I can testify from experience.

Most of the literary agents who advertise for writer clients are, in reality, coaches, rather than manuscript salesmen, and as such are much more interested in the reading and coaching fees they charge than in any possible commissions from sales to publishers. But this *does not* mean that such advertisers are necessarily racketeers.

On the contrary, the able and upstanding ones are doing splendid work. If, as a group, they have sometimes been misunderstood, it is owing to the unethical tactics of a minority and the impossible things that beginning writers often expect of agent-coaches. Writing is a difficult trade; no coach can make a silk purse out of a sow's ear.

No one can turn you into a highly paid professional writer overnight. Nor can you be transformed into a top-flight surgeon or attorney while you sleep. For some curious reason, a seemingly endless procession of simple souls expect coaches to accomplish miracles and feel greatly injured when the miracles do not occur. Before you condemn your coach, recall what you are asking of him.

For a number of years I have been cheerfully "kibitzing" the letters and lessons that conscientious agent-coaches have sent to former or current clients who are also doing work in our non-commercial laboratory. With few exceptions (some, of course, are either fools or knaves), the agent-coaches have revealed an amazingly high level of both quality and quantity of help in return for fees paid. Most frequently, the fault lies with the beginning writer who cannot apply the sound criticism given.

If I were seeking help, I would choose a coach who advertised himself primarily as a coach, rather than as an agent. He would probably turn out to be an honest agent, too.

Generally, the literary agents who are 100 per cent that and nothing else do not advertise, since they have somewhat the same ethic in this respect that doctors and lawyers have. But there are some advertising agents who are all right. I will tell you presently how to find out who they are—both kinds.

As a suggested general procedure, however, do this about your agent or no-agent problem:

(1) Make a genuine effort at first to sell direct. Do not merely send a one story to *The Post* and give up. Study the possible markets; be a little modest about your potential talents, if any; shoot at the magazines you believe you can hit. Fire three, four, five stories, or even more, at a given magazine before you give that one up. And if you get a letter back, or even a brief note, *keep on shooting*.

If an editor takes the trouble to write to you even a few words on the printed rejection slip, patience quite probably will sell him in the end. A few slick magazines, *Esquire* and *Coronet*, for prime examples, apparently send personal rejections with everything returned. This makes for friendship and fine contributor relations. But most editors either cut you off cold with a rejection slip or "see possibilities." If they see possibilities—it is your move next!

(2) After you have sold some stories, ask your editors about agents. Write to the editors of some of the big slick magazines you hope to sell sometime and ask them to recommend one or more firms. They will reply, almost without exception, especially if you enclose return stamps (I think there is a law forbidding editors to use their own stamps), giving you the names and addresses of agents with whom they do business.

And one of these is precisely the agent you want.

(3) Now write to one or two, asking if you may submit a manuscript, inquiring about reading fees, telling where and what you have sold, and so on. If the agent

happens to be an advertising agent, you will know about reading fees from his ads, of course. If you do not know his rules, however, write and ask.

You will find that some agents do and some do not charge reading fees for wading through your stories. Some charge 15 per cent on the first $1,000 of sales in lieu of reading fees. Some will not handle pulp stories, others will, and so on. The typical commission on sales is 10 per cent, incidentally, with usually a somewhat higher fee for sales of additional rights. Pick an agent who seems to suit your needs best.

(4) And, once you have picked an agent, *co-operate with him!* Bear in mind that, if he is to do you the most good, he must become much more than a mere business associate. He will have to be a kind of soul doctor, adviser, friend, coach, and slave driver, all in one. And you will have to bear with him.

You will find, doubtless, that he is even more finicky than the editors, or so it will seem. But if he is worth his salt, he will tell you what he considers to be wrong about stories he returns. Try to improve them in the way he suggests. Do not use another agent at the same time without his knowledge or submit direct to editors. That is, do not send your manuscript direct, unless he does not care to submit the story himself and says so.

Give him a little time in which to get results. Send him as many stories as you can. When he tips you to a possible market, pay attention to his tip. And if he does not write you every day, remember that he doubtless has a few other things to do. He is supposed to sell, not write, anyhow.

(5) Do not expect the agent to sell things you can not sell yourself. (As a matter of fact, he can and will do that very thing *eventually*, if he is experienced and *if you make him like you enough*.) You *can* expect him to widen

your markets—which you could do for yourself, but only at the cost of considerable effort. And you *can* expect him to get your word rates raised—which you might be able to do alone, but, believe me, only with *very* much trouble.

You can expect him to pay his own commissions in those rate boosts alone, if he is knowing and energetic. You can expect him to know about rights, too, and sell some of your secondary rights (matters difficult for the author to handle himself) to your profit and advantage.

(6) But do not sign a contract with him until you are thoroughly satisfied, and, even then, *look over the contract.*

Usually it will be fair. But it could cause you much grief later, were there any unfortunate provisions.

Working Habits.

I have saved this until last because all the things I have been talking about enter into the matter, rather than the manner. This writing craft is not to be learned academically. This book in itself will not do you much good unless and until you absorb, digest, and apply the simplicities it has discussed.

What you have to do is something probably far different from anything you ever did in school. You have to realize that your mind is like a mirror with two surfaces: a shiny, reflecting, front surface, and a dark surface deep down behind.

You have been taught to use mainly the bright, shallow, front surface. Do you remember how many times you memorized in school what you thought would be asked in the examinations, remembered it just long enough to get it down on the examination paper, and then, an hour later, could not recall anything you wrote? Well, that which worked was your intellect, your surface mind. But what you have to do in writing is evoke images from deep down in the dark surface of your subconscious. You know, like in the trick mirrors in which strange images will appear if you breathe upon them just right?

Here are the A B C's of the technique of seeing what other people can't see, making the VP trinity go into action.

(A) *Make a prime habit of writing.*

Check up on the amount of time you can give to your writing, make yourself a schedule, and stick to it.

Until you can make of writing a full-time profession—and don't quit your other job until you are making a living from your stories—don't be too enthusiastic about the amount of time you can devote to your typewriter.

It may not prove so, but expect it to be a long, hard pull. Don't make yourself a schedule calling for fourteen hours a day every day. Even a hardened professional could not maintain such a pace. Writing (good writing) is extremely hard work, probably far different from anything you have ever done before. A four- or five-hour work day usually is the optimum, even for the professional, regardless of his claims of tremendous capacities.

For a beginner, three evenings a week, four evenings, even two evenings are enough, *providing he makes those evenings a fixed habit.*

The idea is, remember, that you are proposing to use a part of your mind you cannot command at will. You have to train it, just as you would a monkey: it cannot be forced to work, but it can be tricked into doing so, persuaded, taught a habit of doing what you want it to do under set circumstances.

Later you will doubtless be able to make your story sense (the subconscious) work at will, anytime and almost anywhere. But in the beginning, while you are training the brute, set for yourself a schedule that you are positive you can keep, then keep it.

(B) *Make it a habit to write a set number of pages at each sitting.*

Occasionally—about twice in a lifetime, say, for the average writer—the subconscious will be showing off, straining at the leash, and the story will come tumbling out as fast as you can write it. At such times, the whole story, perhaps, can be written at one sitting. But this will be a rare experience.

At other times, story consciousness will not work easily and must be poked, prodded, coaxed, cajoled, pushed every inch of the way. This is difficult. Do not make it even more difficult by assigning your story consciousness and yourself an impossible task, a stint of dozens of pages.

You are writing not mere words, but story. Four to eight pages of good story copy are, for most writers, a good day's work. Most writers could write forty pages of mere words in the same time, but they are not writing mere words. Nor should you fail to distinguish between being a stenographer and a writer.

If, as you set out to teach yourself successful writing habits, working from, say, 8 until 11 P.M., you turn out three fairly satisfactory typewritten pages, that isn't bad. Set for yourself an absolute minimum, of, say, two pages and do them, no matter how unsatisfactory they may sound when you have done with them. Do them and do them over and over again, until they sound right. Then, if you still have time, go on to, let us say, a maximum of five pages for the evening's task.

But don't do either too little or too much. The golden mean, that is your ideal. Make it a fixed habit.

(C) *Give yourself a fixed time of day to work.*

Ordinarily, the evening is best as well as most convenient working time for the writer, even the full-time professional. I suggest this because one's own living point-of-the-present, one's life cycle, is moving in the right quadrant between sundown and bedtime. One is traveling then, I mean, from the world of harsh, material, objective fact toward that other world of subjective dreams —precisely the direction most fiction must take.

If, however, you have to work at some other time of day, do not be discouraged. It can be done. Early morning, though, when one is moving in just the wrong direction, from dreamland to cold reality, is the worst time of all. I must admit, however, that I know several quite succesful writers who are perverse enough to do most of their work immediately after early breakfast.

Incidentally, to "look" for your stories just before you go to sleep and just after you wake up is another trick worth teaching yourself. When you are on the border between the two worlds, between fact and fancy, waking and sleeping, you may expect to see best how they link up. Don't "work" at seeing your story at such times; just let it float through your mind. Quite often, you will "see" it suddenly, with no more conscious effort than you would use to turn and look up a street instead of down it.

(D) *Habitually depend on your intuition, your story "feel."*

Which means, in objective action, rewrite until the job is done. Write and rewrite and rewrite again until the thing "feels" right—you do not know precisely why but you know it does! Don't let your intellect trick you into leaving words and sentences in that don't feel, don't belong.

Rewrite your first paragraph, then rewrite it again and again, up to thirty or forty times—until you are entirely satisfied with its *feel*. Pay almost as much attention to your first page as you do to your first paragraph. The first page gives the editor his initial impression, it should be remembered, and the editor acts on the principle that it isn't necessary to eat all of a bad potato in order to know that it is bad.

(E) *Dramatize, dramatize, always dramatize your story.*

Don't become analytical for your reader. It is quite unnecessary to explain the ingredients of your story to him. Put plenty of emotion and action into it, especially in parts 2 and 3, which are hardest for your reader to "see." Don't let your VP character do, see, feel, or think anything that you cannot vividly imagine yourself doing, seeing, feeling, or thinking. For, if you can't put yourself in the position and mood of the VP character, you can't put the reader there, either. Go all out on your decision, sacrifice, black moment, and reward.

You can always boil down or cut back description which is too emotional. That is relatively easy. But if it doesn't have "kick" to begin with, you are in a bad way.

(F) *Always keep a notebook.*

And keep it handy! Jot down a few words to preserve story ideas whenever they strike you. Write down neat phrases, ways to say things that impress you, quotations you like, and so on. Keep the notebook near your bed, so that even in the dark you can reach out and make a few scribbles to hold the story until morning.

(G) *And finally, make it your unvarying habit to finish every story you start.*

The reason for this is that, somewhere along the line in every story, the writer reaches his own personal Black Moment. Pouring out from his own mind onto white paper the emotional power, the tremendous "kick" of his story, he inevitably exhausts himself as the story sweeps on to its close. The better he is accomplishing his task on paper, ordinarily, the blacker will be his personal Black Moment when he reaches it. *But, if he lets this increasing depression and weariness persuade him to quit, he may stop two pages short of a supreme triumph, a masterpiece.*

Don't do it! Don't confuse work and play. The mere fact that you like to read gives you no reason to believe that you should like to write. You have to pay for books or magazines, don't you, whereas if you do it right, you get paid for writing? This world pays you to work, charges you to play. Therefore, always finish your story no matter how sorry it may seem to you on page 14. Perhaps the editor will have an opinion different from yours. If he does, you will enjoy what he writes, namely, a check.

~~ VI ~~

Analyses of Stories

LIKE the Greek poet Hesiod, of the eighth century, B.C., I have a feeling that things, particularly stories, were better in my youth. Perhaps they were; perhaps also I had more enthusiasm and eagerness, so that everything appeared more glamorous then. Even so, the basic pattern persists, now as then. The judgment of values, the philosophy behind the fiction, seems to have weakened. But perhaps as Hesiod always said, "Now when I was young..."

Here, for examples, are the plots of short stories published recently in seven assorted national magazines. In revising this chapter fifteen years after writing the original, I have discovered one significant fact: there is increased difficulty in deciding whether the decision is "plus" or "minus," the answer "good" or "bad." In a century in which moral values are fading like yesterday's flowers, this inability to tell the difference between good and evil, this attempt to accommodate and tolerate both, is doubtless to be expected. The arithmetical pattern of the short story, however, remains unchanged.

The Saturday Evening Post
August 2, 1958

I selected this issue, frankly, because it contains stories by two University of Oklahoma professional writing graduates, the lead story by the late Mary Agnes Thompson and the fourth tale by Ed Montgomery. Four short stories in this issue, two $1 + 1$, one $1 - 1$, and one doubtful.

"Bachelor's Choice," by Mary Agnes Thompson. Story equation: *love + loyalty = ?*

Tone Hrdlicka, a young Czech farmer, has never married, largely because he fears any wife will promptly throw Old Svec, the hired man, out. Old Svec has been with the Hrdlickas all Tone's life and Tone is fiercely loyal to him, even though the old man's cooking has been terrible of late. But now a crisis has arisen.

It is harvest time and the crew has complained about the poor food. Tone hires four women cooks, or rather three cooks and one gorgeous cookie, Karolina Bukovnik, who can't even peel potatoes and is defiant about it to boot.

Each of the other three women cooks a meal for the harvest hands; then they announce that it is Karolina's turn and they won't help her. Old Svec volunteers his assistance, and, although the hands object, Tone (decision) tells him to go ahead. He pays off his other three cooks, fully expecting the worst.

The meal is excellent, Czech cooking at its best. Karolina confesses she didn't cook it—Svec did—and declares that nobody else but Svec is going to teach her to cook. This solves Tone's problem. Svec confesses that his cooking has been bad on purpose—to persuade Tone to marry. Tone proposes to Karolina. She says yes, and adds that Mama made her come in order to find a husband. But Tone must keep Svec—to which Tone solemnly agrees.

Comment: Full of warm color. Note how each character has a problem, all tied to the central issue, Tone's getting married.

"Forbidden Hours," by MacDonald Harris. Story equation: *pride — love = ?*

Jonathan Lyle meets a beautiful, mysterious sixteen-year-old girl, Martha, quite informally at a pier and takes her sailing in his little boat. They fall in love. Then when she confesses that she is a movie star, he tells her stiffly (decision) he'll see her in the movies and she replies she'll see him in the funny papers.

Comment: Approaches literary story pattern.

"A Highly Ridiculous Animal," by Brian Cleeve. Story equation: *love — honesty = ?*

An Irish lad, Mike (I suppose; his name is never made clear), proposes to steal a valuable dog from some visiting Americans and enter him in a coursing match, to win enough money to run away. He uses his own dog, Sally, to lure the prize hound off. But the officials of the match refuse to believe the stolen dog is a hound at all, laugh at him, and won't even let him enter the match. Mike returns the dog and is at first praised for "finding" the valuable animal (an Arabian Saluki); then, when the truth comes out, is sternly reprimanded and sent home. Later Sally has a pup which looks just like the prize Saluki.

Comment: Typically Irish story, full of lovely, vague sentiment that doesn't add up to much of anything. Note that there is a "wrong" decision (to steal the dog) which leads to an unhappy answer (failure to get into the match and subsequent detection as a thief) and a "right" decision (to take the dog back), followed by a happy answer (the pup which looks just like the prize dog).

"Devil in the Brush," by Ed Montgomery. Story equation: *love + safety = ?*

Will Applewhite, former convict, who got caught by the law while sleeping in a house, won't go into one any more. He lives like a wild man, hunting and trapping. He meets Mary Martha Barnes, girl owner of the local produce house, and falls in love with her. Also he discovers that an old acquaintance, Gilliland, an escaped convict and murderer, is in the area and has found out that he (Will) has money.

Learning that Martha is in financial difficulties, Will tries to help her out. He proposes to her (decision), and Martha comes out to his woodland retreat to see how he lives. Gilliland has come out, too, intending to attack and rob Will. Will gets him with an improvised shotgun slug and decides he'll swallow his fears and try living in a house again, with Martha.

Comment: Interesting bit of technical information in this, how to make a deadly big-game slug out of a bird-shot shell.

McCall's
September, 1959

This is the "togetherness" magazine, for women. Five short stories in this issue, all 1 + 1.

"Double Wedding," by Adela Rogers St. Johns. Story equation: *pride + love = ?*

Schatzi Criandos is snubbed by her sister, Babs, because Schatzi has married millions, while Babs married poor. Schatzi's offer to buy a pair of orthopedic shoes for Babs' little boy, Panky, is haughtily refused.

Emotionally disturbed, Schatzi is involved in a car wreck. She comes back, somewhat battered and wailing (decision) that she wants to be loved even with money. So Babs, in one of those truly bitter decisions found often in women's magazine stories, announces that she does love Schatzi and her money too.

Comment: You will notice that this "Love me, love my money" happy answer varies somewhat from the stern Biblical precept that the love of money is the root of all evil.

"Could Happen to Any Man," by Willard Temple. Story equation: *pride + love = ?*

Walter expects to spend some lonely nights at home while his wife, Helen, is in the hospital recovering from an appendectomy. Instead, he is entertained by a redhead; by an elderly friend with a young wife; by a neighbor couple who quarrel, the husband leaving Walter to squire the attractive wife; and by four friends who stay all night to play poker. Walter doesn't tell Helen about any of this, but she comes home unexpectedly, learns all, and puts him out of the house after announcing she is going to divorce him. He sprains an ankle trying to force his way back into his house, finds his wife is having lunch with her lawyer, and starts for his hotel to launch divorce proceedings himself (decision), only to be met at the door by a penitent Helen, who has heard how innocent he really is.

Comment: When husband decides to sacrifice love for pride and leave wife, a reversal of his previous stand, this permits wife to reverse also and persuade him to stay. Neat story mechanics, though probably not very true to real life.

"The Little Lady and the Chairman of the Board," by Robert W. Wells. Story equation: *obstinacy + reasonableness = ?*

Alice Carstairs, who has tried vainly to find solitude everywhere else, has bought a lot in the middle of the city's business district and now demands that the Pipp Tower Corporation move its thirty-three-story skyscraper eighteen inches off her lot, so that she can build a ranch-type home and be peaceful in the middle of the maddening crowd. Meek little Everett Glinchy, board member, solves the problem by persuading her to accept a building site atop the skyscraper, where she can find real peace.

Comment: Nicely done humorous story, employing the usual basis for humor, simple reversal. When he finds he can't move the determined heroine, Mr. Glinchy simply moves her building site.

"Roulette," by Alma Scott. Story equation: *personal triumph + love = ?*

In Reno with her husband, Carl, on a business trip, Janet takes advantage of a few hours alone to gamble and wins over $700 at roulette. When she meets her husband, he is excited about making a good sale. In order not to dim his moment of triumph, Janet (decision) keeps still about her own.

Comment: The thesis of women's magazines is that men must be coddled. Note that a negative decision, i.e., not to do something, is quite often encountered in women's stories. In stories for males the decisions usually are positive, to do something.

"Wives of the Year," by Marnie Ellingson. Story equation: *fear + love = ?*

The heroine, not named, is one of a team sent by *Hearthside Magazine* to choose Mrs. Eagle Falls of 1959. She loves Pete, the staff photographer, but is afraid she's such a poor cook and housekeeper she wouldn't make him a good wife. She discovers that Molly Cummings, one of the contestants, had the same fear before she married. At each test Molly puts her family first, even deciding to serve the test dinner to a relative who chances to visit. Molly's husband and family obviously adore her. The magazine team votes Molly the award, and the heroine decides she will take a chance with Pete.

Comment: Best story in the issue for my money, because this one has food value. It tells the housewife reader how to make use of her greatest strength.

Harper's

August, 1959

This is a literary magazine. Two stories, one a wry, hesitant $1 + 1$ and the other $1 - 1$, in the usual literary manner.

"The Case for Mr. Parkhill," by Leo Rosten. Story equation: *gratitude + snobbishness = ?*

On his birthday Mr. Parkhill, who would much prefer teaching in an exclusive private school, is being made miserable by the illiterate conversation of the immigrants in his class in the Night Preparatory School for Adults. They present him with an attaché case, initialed "M.P." For a moment Mr. Parkhill is puzzled, until suddenly he realizes, with gratification, that the letters stand for "Mr. Parkhill," the only name they know for him.

Comment: The real decision, in proper literary plot style, obviously is in the past, when Mr. Parkhill decided to remain a mere night school teacher instead of trying for a position in a high-class private academy. Now he is unhappy about it, though it is faintly pleasing to discover that his crude students do not consider him one of them, that they think of him only as a formal "Mister."

"A Wild Night in Galway," by Ray Bradbury. Story equation: *expectation − realization = ?*

Half-frozen and bored stiff while working on a Mexican bullfight script in wintry Ireland, the unnamed hero accepts Pubkeeper Johnny Murphy's invitation to a wild Irish night (decision). The entertainment turns out to be a dreary, rain-drenched, illicit dog race. Thoroughly disillusioned, the hero returns to his room.

Comment: Unless the author is saying, "Don't expect the Irish to produce much," I don't know what this is all about.

Argosy
July, 1959

This is a leading men's magazine. Four short stories in this issue, all $1 + 1$. Notice that love is not one of the emotions involved in any of the equations.

"Trouble in the Stokehole," by George Poulin. Story equation: *fear + brashness = ?*

Francis O'Toole, incorrigible boilerman first class, jumps ship for a date. Accidentally he becomes involved in a kidnapping and gets back aboard ship with a baby, the infant King of Leberan. Afraid to tell the skipper, O'Toole has all sorts of fantastic troubles caring for the baby on a navy ship. Then the admiral comes for inspection. O'Toole (decision) hides the baby in the skipper's cabin and then finesses the incredibly stupid admiral into praising him for saving the baby and keeping the nation out of a serious controversy.

Comment: Pretty incredible, but here it is.

"Setup for Dying," by Norman Daniels. Story equation: *Respect for life + fear = ?*

Bert Larkin, wartime triggerman now running a gun shop in America, is approached by a blackmailing wartime acquaintance, Paul, who threatens exposure unless Bert ambushes a certain enemy of Paul's as the man leaves his office building. At the appointed time Bert's wife visits Paul in his office, hands him a notched bullet, opens the curtains, and informs him that Bert is in a building across the street with a telescopic sight trained on him. If he moves, he will be killed. Then she leaves. The decision, offstage, is to risk exposure and not kill the proposed victim.

Comment: This decision, alas, doesn't solve anything, since the blackmailer presumably would go ahead and expose Bert unless Bert killed him first. The story suffers also from being too long, going on to reveal that Bert doesn't even have his rifle with him, only his telescopic sight. Thus Paul is not in real danger. Since readers usually feel cheated when a danger they accepted as real proves phony, it is a good rule always to run this the other way. A seemingly phony danger may prove to be real, but a seemingly real one should never prove to be false.

"The Empty Glass," by Fred McMorrow. Story equation: *grief + courage = ?*

"Gunner" Boyle, a hoodlum, is to be electrocuted for murder at 11:00 P.M. His good brother, Jim, sits in a bar, buying drinks for all hands until 11:00, when he breaks an empty glass with his bare hands for Gunner, as his brother had asked.

Comment: Decision is to stay and break the glass. Just misses being a very good story.

"The Night of the Killer," by Jack Schaefer. Story equation: *courage + wisdom = ?*

Old Ramon, a sheepherder, gives a dog, Sancho, to his *patrón*'s young son, who is helping him for experience. In the night a wolf attacks the flock. Pedro, an old dog, comes to get the sheepherders (decision) while Sancho stays to fight the wolf and is killed. The boy calls Pedro a coward, but Ramon denies it, saying Pedro was wise, and as for bravery, Pedro once attacked a bear and saved his (Ramon's) life.

Comment: This is an example of accommodating a city man's morals to a country story, a technique at which this author is very adept and successful. *The Virginian*, by Owen Wister, perhaps the most famous Western ever written, is another instance of the same technique. In my opinion, the old dog's behavior is not admirable, and

Ramon's assertion that the old dog was brave once does not justify his running away now, nor is it convincing, since it is telling, not showing.

True Story
July, 1959

This is a confession-story magazine, one of a group which serves more than twenty million readers. This field demands highly emotional, dramatic plots and, despite hostile criticism in some quarters, is thus, in my opinion, one of the best training grounds possible for aspiring writers. Four short stories in this issue, plus three "long stories" (novelettes), plus an article on artificial insemination done in short story form, an interesting novelty.

"Take Care of Her While I'm Gone." Story equation: *love + self-interest = ?*

A lusty young wench, Lynne, is afraid she is "bad" because of her vigorous sex impulses. She marries a cold man, Alan, who neglects her and gives her no satisfaction. In time she meets another man, Ray, has an affair with him, and really falls in love. Alan discovers her infidelity and is coldly furious, but he won't give her a divorce and threatens to ruin her reputation if she tries to divorce him. Finally (decision) she tells Alan she is going to the other man regardless of consequences. Alan relents and lets her go.

Comment: Pretty poor plotting here in that the story attempts to justify self-indulgence on the part of the heroine, though it is "wrong" on the part of the husband! But the plot pattern of problem, decision, and reversal to attain an answer is present.

"Boys Talk about Girls like Me." Story equation: *romanticism + honesty = ?*

Norma is a lonely teen-ager with bad teeth. She gets them fixed and promptly starts off on a spree. She meets a nice boy, is seduced by the villain, runs away from a wild party, and, when she is found, accuses the nice boy of raping her. Then (decision) she repents and tells the truth, thus smearing herself. But now she has learned, and there's another boy . . .

Comment: "Come to realize" is a favorite theme in confessions. It is not the best plotting, because few people ever do "come to realize" error except with a specific example in front of them, one they can see. Thus, in this instance, if some other girl had accused the boy of rape and the heroine knew it was not true but would have to reveal the fact she was at the wild party too (and thus damage her own reputation) by coming forward to tell the truth, we might possibly have a better plot. It is easier for us to see someone else's error. But "come to realize" will sell, if well done, in almost any market.

"At the End of Her Rope," by Sarah Plummer. Story equation: *freedom + responsibility = ?*

This is a novelty in the confessions, a signed story told by a Children's Aid homemaker. Confessions, of course, usually are anonymous. Sent to help in the unhappy home of Naomi and Mel, Mrs. Plummer finds Naomi a malcontent determined to learn nothing, shoulder no responsibility for her family, and accept nothing but her "freedom." Eventually Naomi runs away, but when she finds out how shabby the jobs she could get really are, she decides she wants her family and husband, even with the responsibilities.

Comment: Nicely done.

"Living It Up." Story equation: *thoughtless pleasure + responsibility = ?*

Patty and Jimmy, a young married couple, are running with a wild set. One week end they both get drunk, flirt with other partners, and have a drunken fight. Patty ends in a hospital, where she finds she has lost the baby she didn't even know was coming, while Jimmy is being fined in police court. They repent (decision), abandon their wild ways, and discover that more conventional living is better.

Comment: Another "come to realize." The formula demanded by most confession editors is, as here, "sin, suffer, and repent." Other confession editors prefer to call sin a "character flaw." Regardless of terminology, an emotional problem must confront the central character and be resolved by decision and action.

Famous Western
October, 1959

The once flourishing Western pulp magazines are in sad estate today, almost gone from the American publishing scene. I predict they will some day make a comeback, since the Western is the American folk saga, our version of the old miracle play. Four short stories in this issue.

"A Gunslick Pays Out," by Wallace McKinley. Story equation: *courage + fear = ?*

"Calamity" Kaine, gambler, shows up in a town where the sheriff is being buffaloed by a bully gang topped by "Bloody Jim" Wills, lightning gunman. Kaine pretends to be drunk, lets them entice him into a rigged game, calls their hand (decision), and neatly shoots all five of the gang! This last, you understand, is why I call Westerns miracle stories.

Comment: In an age which no longer believes in miracles, the miracle stories seem pretty sad. But the pattern is here.

"Ride the Texas Wonder," by D. L. Hyde. Story equation: *pride + honesty = ?*

This is really a novelette, two short stories rolled together. The Wagon Tongue and the Diamond O outfits tangle in a rodeo contest. "Tenderfoot" Winston wins the bucking horse contest and (decision) confesses later he isn't really a tenderfoot—he has been riding all his life. Lafe wins the donkey race and (decision) confesses he used a miracle glue to hold him in the saddle.

Comment: There's that miracle again.

"Sermon in Lead," by Olin Grant. Story equation: *courage + fear = ?*

The Reverend Oderley starts to clean up Silver City, pretty much run by Jamie Guest, saloonkeeper. At Jamie's instigation some cowpunchers try to make the preacher dance, and shoot into the church. The parson gets a gun and (decision) shoots all the bottles off the shelves in Jamie's saloon. Jamie is laughed into giving in.

Comment: This isn't quite as unbelievable as it sounds. After all, Carry Nation used to take her hatchet and do just this to Western saloonkeepers, and she got away with it.

"The Bell Tolls to Murder," by Harlan Clay. Story equation: *courage + fear = ?*

Sheriff Sumpter Gray is trying to drink himself to death. He is rescued from a blizzard by Eve Tarrant, who has had a mysterious church bell left in her charge by Preacher Kirk. The villainous Greer brothers kill Eve's father, crease Gray, and steal the bell, which (so a letter from the preacher now reveals) turns out to be one of three cast for Emperor Maximilian of Mexico, in one of which the crown jewels were hidden. Sumpter (decision) takes on all three of the Greers singlehanded, including the toughest, in a rip-roaring Bowie knife fight. He wins (miracle!), and the bell is recovered. But it is not the one with the jewels.

Comment: Colorful detail. Westerns should be larger than life size. Western authors, however, should learn that even villains, in 1866, did not shoot Winchester .30–.30's, a caliber not produced until 1894.

Ellery Queen's Mystery Magazine
October, 1959

A detective, or mystery, story is aimed at a reader much more flat-minded, objective, and materialistic than the typical reader of, say, love stories or even Westerns. The basic pattern of problem, decision and action, answer remains, the detective character usually betting his life, reputation, job, or commission that he is right in his deduction. But the emphasis is on reasoning, the intellectual ability to see the connection between tangible parts. Thus knowledge of minutiae, as for instance that English telephone dials are different from American, used in "English Lesson," by Ernest Harrison, in this issue, becomes valuable information for an aspiring writer of detective stories. Nine short stories in this magazine.

"The Day of the Bullet," by Stanley Ellin. Story equation: *self-interest — honor = ?*

This is a "minus" story. The narrator, reading that Ignace Kovacs, Brooklyn rackets boss, has been murdered, remembers the day, years before, when he and Iggy saw a local racketeer beat up a victim and toss him into a pond. When Iggy insisted on reporting the affair to the police, the cops wouldn't believe him; the racketeer, brought in, blandly denied the story, and Iggy's father, intimidated, ordered the boy not to tell such stories about people. So (decision and reversal) Iggy decided he would tell the racketeer on his father if the old man ever tried anything.

Comment: Circumstances persuade the boy that an honorable course is stupid—a dishonest one profitable, in other words. Eventually he ends as a racketeer and gang victim himself.

"There's Still Tomorrow," by George Harmon Coxe. Story equation: *fear + intellectual confidence = ?*

Alan Marsh finds a nude, unconscious, possibly dying girl in the bathroom of a friend's apartment. He is suspected of being the assailant but proves a woman visitor is guilty, because puddles on the floor show that the victim stepped out of the shower to talk with the intruder, which she wouldn't have done had it been a man. Moreover, although it is now raining outside, the assailant's suit is unspotted, so she couldn't have arrived at the time she claimed she did.

Comment: The decision, of course, is where the detective character puts the finger on the criminal, says, "Youdunnit," and then proceeds to explain how he knows.

"The Case of the Blue Bowl," by E. X. Ferrars. Story equation: *fear + intellectual confidence = ?*

An old lady is found murdered. Her nephew is suspected. The hero proves the milkman is the murderer, however, because the blue bowl put over the milk bottle on the step—to keep the birds from getting at the milk— is a rare Chinese antique, and the nephew, an antique dealer, would never have used such a valuable object in this way.

Comment: Note how the author puts together seemingly trivial minutiae. I wasn't smart enough to see possibilities when I read about people having to put cups over milk bottles to stop milk-stealing birds—even though I had heard the story about the antique dealer who sold seven worthless cats to "smart" antique china collectors by feeding the kittens milk from a very rare saucer at his front door. The smart boys would buy the cat, try to take the saucer, too—and discover they'd been had. Ah, well, one can't see everything.

"The Moonlight Gunner," by Arthur Gordon. Story equation: *fear + courage = ?*

In this one the mysterious pretty lady persuades the black market duck hunter to take her out to a duck blind and there accuses him of having murdered a warden. He brazenly admits the deed after slapping the gun out of her hands. On shore, confronted by the sheriff, he denies having admitted the murder. But the lady, the game warden's widow, had a tape recorder hidden in her shell box.

Comment: Pretty dumb gunner.

"The Simple Solution," by Nicholas DiMinno. Story equation: *reputation + intellectual confidence = ?*

A police lieutenant is detailed to trace down the missing wife of a writer, Benedict Blake. The lieutenant thinks she has been murdered, but Blake, with a broken foot in a cast, obviously could not have disposed of the body. Finally the lieutenant traces down the very first book written by Blake, which relates an exactly similar situation, in which the body was buried in the basement. He examines the Blake basement, and, sure enough, there is the body.

Comment: But I still don't see how a man with a foot in a cast could carry a body clear down to the basement and even do cement work!

"English Lesson," by Ernest Harrison. Story equation: *doubt + intellectual confidence = ?*

An English jewel thief claims that he was in the United States at the time of a theft. Scotland Yard says he has never been out of England. The professor proves the thief is lying by having him make some calls on an American phone, which he uses in the English fashion. Had he ever visited the U.S.A. and used a telephone, as he claims, he would have learned that our phones have a letter "O," which the English phones lack, and that we dial two letters of the exchange.

Comment: It's the little things that count.

"The Unique Guinea," by Stephen Barr. Story equation: *fear + self-possession = ?*

A host at a dinner party tells the story of a counterfeit guinea struck for Bonnie Prince Charlie, the Young Pretender, in an abortive plan to embarrass the English with spurious money. The plan was abandoned and, so far as he knows, he has the only coin struck. After he shows it, it vanishes from the table. All the guests agree to turn out their pockets save one, who insists on further search of the room. Reluctantly the diners agree, and the missing coin is found where it had rolled into a crack. Then the suspect explains why he wouldn't agree to be searched: He has in his pocket a second golden guinea identical to the first, given to an ancestor by Prince Charlie's mistress.

Comment: Clever. You swallow the whopping coincidence of the two coins at the same party easily.

"D. A.'s Dream Case," by Alex Gaby. Story equation: *fear + intellectual confidence = ?*

This is really the murderer's story. A shot is heard just as Sunday church service is concluding, and a gambler is found dead with old Frank Ruppert sitting beside him holding a smoking gun. The district attorney, Floyd Mellis, who hates Ruppert, hastens his murder trial. But at the trial, after all evidence places the time of the killing at one o'clock, the coroner's report, which the overly hasty district attorney hasn't read completely, establishes the fact the gambler had been dead for more than two hours at that time. The charge is faulty, the case is dismissed, and Ruppert cannot be tried again, even though, as he later admits, he did kill the gambler in mid-morning (the villain was about to seduce the old man's granddaughter). He then waited until one, when he knew it would be heard, to fire a second shot up the chimney. He was sure the district attorney wouldn't read all the coroner's report, and the doctor, an old friend, wouldn't volunteer any help.

Comment: More a character story than a detective yarn.

"Open Verdict," by Gerald Kersh. Story equation: *fear — intellectual confidence = ?*

This is a sort of minus version of the "moonlight gunner" plot above. In this one an old lady is murdered in a locked bedroom with only an eight-year-old niece in the room. She has been killed by an embroidery needle driven through her skull, an incredible feat of strength and skill, seemingly quite impossible for a child. But the hapless detective finds a book of tricks in the room, including instructions for driving a needle through a penny by first sticking the needle through a cork and then hitting it with a hammer. He accuses the child, who blithely admits the murder, then cries and denies all before witnesses in the police station. So—since he didn't have a tape recorder—they believe the girl and fire the policeman.

Comment: You can find good detective minutiae almost anywhere, even in a child's book of tricks. The idea of the child murderer is reminiscent of the popular play, *The Bad Seed.*

And now, I think I have gone quite far enough with these formulas and synopses.

Try them for yourself with any fiction magazines at hand. Don't be troubled if it takes a bit of time to "see" the equations, or if you cannot state them as precisely as you might wish. Remember, these are, after all, subjective mathematics and as such are not matters of precise, objective definition. If you can sense and approximate such problems as *pride+love* and *greed—honor*, that is enough, because you have acquired the basic ability to "see" story. And that, in the final analysis, is what you are after.

"Seeing" the pattern on which other stories are built is the first long step toward seeing and beginning to build successful, selling stories of your own. Good hunting!

University of Oklahoma Press : Norman